Life Promises for Couples

LIFE PROMISES
for Couples

God's promises for you and your spouse

GARY CHAPMAN

Bestselling author of *The Five Love Languages*

Tyndale House Publishers, Inc. • Carol Stream, Illinois

Visit Tyndale online at www.tyndale.com.

TYNDALE and Tyndale's quill logo are registered trademarks of Tyndale House Publishers, Inc.

Life Promises for Couples: God's Promises for You and Your Spouse

Some material selected from The One Year Love Language Minute Devotional, copyright © 2009 by Gary D. Chapman.

Designed by Jacqueline L. Nuñez

Library of Congress Cataloging-in-Publication Data

Chapman, Gary D., date.
  Life promises for couples : God's promises for you and your spouse / Gary Chapman.
      p. cm.
  Includes index.
  ISBN 978-1-4143-6391-2 (hc)
  1. Marriage—Religious aspects—Christianity. 2. Spouses—Religious life. I. Title.
BV4596.M3C483 2011
248.8'44—dc23   2011027476

Printed in China

17   16   15   14   13   12   11
7   6   5   4   3   2   1

Introduction

I've been privileged to counsel couples for more than thirty years, and in that time I've seen my share of marital struggles. But what I've also seen, time and time again, is the power of God to transform relationships. When two people commit to each other—and especially when they commit to communicating love to each other through the five love languages—positive change occurs.

Because my background is in marriage counseling, I tend to use the language of marriage when I write. Some of the issues I address are marriage specific. However, if you're a dating or engaged couple, I hope you will read this book too. There is plenty of helpful information for you as well. The building blocks of marriage—such as good communication, respect, unconditional love, and forgiveness—are foundational to any romantic relationship. And learning to identify and speak your loved one's love language will benefit a couple at any stage.

You can use this Bible promise book individually, or sit down as a couple and read it together. In just a minute or two every day, you can discover encouraging biblical insights.

Whether your relationship is strong or struggling, stable or challenging, my prayer is that this little book will encourage you and give you renewed joy in each other. May your relationship be strengthened as you focus on loving and growing together.

Gary Chapman

Life Promises

Three things will last forever—faith, hope, and love—and
the greatest of these is love. Let love be your highest goal!

1 CORINTHIANS 13:13–14:1

Dear friends, since God loved us that much, we surely ought
to love each other. No one has ever seen God. But if we love
each other, God lives in us, and his love is brought to full
expression in us.

1 JOHN 4:11–12

I am giving you a new commandment: Love each other.
Just as I have loved you, you should love each other. Your
love for one another will prove to the world that you are
my disciples.

JOHN 13:34-35

The Language of Love

After thirty years of counseling couples, I'm convinced there are five different ways we speak and understand emotional love—five love languages.

- · Words of affirmation—using positive words to affirm the one you love
- · Gifts—giving thoughtful gifts to show you were thinking about someone
- · Acts of service—doing something that you know the other person would like
- · Quality time—giving your undivided attention
- · Physical touch—holding hands, kissing, embracing, or any other affirming touch

Each of us has a primary love language. One of these five languages speaks to us more profoundly than the other four.

Seldom, however, do a husband and wife have the same love language. We tend to speak our own language, and as a result, we completely miss each other. Oh, we're sincere. We're even expressing love, but we're not connecting emotionally.

Sound familiar? Love doesn't need to diminish over time. The end of the famous "love chapter" of the Bible, I Corinthians 13, says that love is of great value and will last forever. In fact, the apostle Paul says that love should be our highest goal. But if you're going to keep love alive, you need to learn a new language—your loved one's language.

That takes discipline and practice—but the reward is a lasting, deeply committed relationship.

Life Promises

Whatever you wish that others would do to you, do also to them, for this is the Law and the Prophets.

MATTHEW 7:12, ESV

Let us not love in word or talk but in deed and in truth.

1 JOHN 3:18, ESV

See what kind of love the Father has given to us, that we should be called children of God; and so we are.

1 JOHN 3:1, ESV

How May I Help You?

The word *Christian* means "Christlike." In the first century, *Christian* was not a name chosen by the followers of Jesus. Rather, it was a name given to them by others. Believers based their lifestyle on the teachings of Christ, so the best way to describe them was to call them Christians.

What if Christians really were Christlike? Central in Jesus' teachings is the command to love. In fact, in Mark 12:29-31, Jesus said that the greatest commandment is to love God and the second is to love our neighbors. These commands supersede all others, because everything else flows out from them.

Love begins with an attitude, which in turn leads to acts of service. How may I help you? is a good question with which to begin.

Today is a good day to express love to our neighbors. In my opinion, that starts with those closest to us—first our spouse, then our family—and then spreads outward.

Life Promises

All of us who have had that veil removed can see and reflect the glory of the Lord. And the Lord—who is the Spirit— makes us more and more like him as we are changed into his glorious image.

2 CORINTHIANS 3:18

The LORD directs the steps of the godly. He delights in every detail of their lives.

PSALM 37:23

Seek his will in all you do, and he will show you which path to take.

PROVERBS 3:6

The Big Reveal

What do you know about the art of self-revelation? It all began with God. God revealed himself to us through the prophets, the Scriptures, and supremely through Christ.

The same principle is necessary in marriage. Self-revelation enables us to get to know each other's ideas, desires, frustrations, and joys. In a word, it is the road to intimacy. No self-revelation, no intimacy. So how do we learn the art of self-revelation?

You can begin by learning to speak for yourself. Communication experts often explain it as using "I" statements rather than "you" statements. For example, "*I* feel disappointed that you are not going with me to my mother's birthday dinner" is very different from "*You* have disappointed me again by not going to my mother's birthday dinner."

When you focus on your reaction, you reveal your own emotions. Focusing on the other person's actions places blame. "You" statements encourage arguments. "I" statements encourage communication.

Life Promises

Honesty guides good people; dishonesty destroys treacherous people.

PROVERBS 11:3

For everything there is a season, a time for every activity under heaven. . . . A time to cry and a time to laugh. A time to grieve and a time to dance. . . . A time to embrace and a time to turn away. . . . A time to tear and a time to mend. A time to be quiet and a time to speak.

ECCLESIASTES 3:1, 4, 5, 7

Get rid of all bitterness, rage, anger, harsh words, and slander, as well as all types of evil behavior. Instead, be kind to each other, tenderhearted, forgiving one another, just as God through Christ has forgiven you.

EPHESIANS 4:31-32

Express Yourself!

Some people wonder why they would ever want to share their feelings with their mate. The truth is, if you don't openly share your feelings, they will likely show up anyway in your behavior. However, your loved one will have no idea why you are behaving as you are. That's when you get the classic question, Is something wrong? Your spouse knows something is wrong but doesn't know what.

Emotions are a natural part of life. King Solomon writes in Ecclesiastes that there is a time for everything, including joy and sorrow, grieving and celebration. All feelings have their place in our lives, and many of them communicate a lot about us. Most of our feelings are tied to some experience we have had in the past or something we're going through now. The next time you feel disappointed, ask yourself, "What stimulated my disappointment?" Then try to share whatever it is with your spouse.

Revealing your feelings lets your spouse know what is going on inside you—what you are feeling and why. For example, you might say, "I'm feeling angry with myself because I came home late last night and we missed our ride in the country." Such a statement may encourage your mate to say, "I'm disappointed too. Maybe we can do it on Thursday night." Revealing your feelings creates an atmosphere of intimacy and trust.

Life Promises

[Jesus said,] "Why worry about a speck in your friend's eye when you have a log in your own? . . . First get rid of the log in your own eye; then you will see well enough to deal with the speck in your friend's eye."

MATTHEW 7:3, 5

Though the LORD is great, he cares for the humble, but he keeps his distance from the proud.

PSALM 138:6

Do nothing from rivalry or conceit, but in humility count others more significant than yourselves.

PHILIPPIANS 2:3, ESV

Time for a Change

As a marriage counselor, I've drawn one conclusion: everyone wishes his or her spouse would change. "We could have a good marriage if he would just help me more around the house." Or "Our marriage would be great if she was willing to have sex more than once a month." He wants her to change, and she wants him to change. The result? Both feel condemned and resentful.

Jesus' words in Matthew 7 vividly illustrate the problem. We think we see others' faults clearly, and we put forth a lot of effort to try to correct them. But in reality, our own sin blinds us. If we haven't dealt with our own failings, we have no business criticizing our spouse's.

There is a better way: start with yourself. Admit that you're not perfect. Confess some of your most obvious failures to your spouse and acknowledge that you want to change. Ask for one suggestion each week on how you could be a better husband or wife. To the best of your ability, make changes. Chances are, your spouse will reciprocate.

Life Promises

[John the Baptist's] message was, "Repent of your sins and turn to God, for the Kingdom of Heaven is near. . . . Prove by the way you live that you have repented of your sins and turned to God."

MATTHEW 3:1-2, 8

If my people who are called by my name will humble themselves and pray and seek my face and turn from their wicked ways, I will hear from heaven and will forgive their sins.

2 CHRONICLES 7:14

If we confess our sins to him, he is faithful and just to forgive us our sins and to cleanse us from all wickedness.

1 JOHN 1:9

Time for a You-Turn

A woman said to me recently, "We have the same old arguments about the same old things. We've been married for thirty years, and I'm sick of his apologies. I want him to change." This woman wanted her husband to repent. The word *repentance* means "to turn around." In the context of an apology, it means that I deeply regret the pain my behavior has caused, and I choose to change my behavior.

John the Baptist preached that people needed to repent—to turn away from their sins and turn toward God. When Jesus began his ministry, he had the same message. The proof of our heart change is in our actions. When Christ rules in our hearts, we are not happy to keep repeating the same old sins. Instead, we reach out for divine help to change our ways.

When we hurt our spouse, we must acknowledge that what we have done is wrong and that just apologizing is not enough to make it right. We also need to make a plan to change our actions so we don't hurt our loved one in the same way again. Why would we not want to do that in our closest relationship? Repentance is a vital part of a genuine apology.

Life Promises

Repent, and turn from your sins. Don't let them destroy you! Put all your rebellion behind you, and find yourselves a new heart and a new spirit.

EZEKIEL 18:30-31

If anyone is in Christ, he is a new creation. The old has passed away; behold, the new has come.

2 CORINTHIANS 5:17, ESV

God did what the law could not do. He sent his own Son in a body like the bodies we sinners have. And in that body God declared an end to sin's control over us by giving his Son as a sacrifice for our sins.

ROMANS 8:3

Seeing Is Believing

All of us need to learn to apologize, for one simple reason: we are all sinners. From time to time we all hurt the people we love the most. When we apologize, we hope the person we have offended will forgive us. We can make that easier if we include in our apology a statement of repentance or change. As one woman said, "I don't want to just hear words; I want to see changes. When he indicates that he intends to change, I'm always willing to forgive him."

All true repentance begins in the heart. The decision to change shows that we are no longer making excuses or minimizing our behavior. Instead, we are accepting full responsibility for our actions. As Scripture says, we are putting our sinful behavior behind us and seeking "a new heart and a new spirit" (Ezekiel 18:31). Only God can give those. He can renew in us a desire to change the way we act. He can help us do better. When we share our desire to change, the offended party gets a glimpse of our heart. That often leads to forgiveness.

Life Promises

Two people are better off than one, for they can help each other succeed. If one person falls, the other can reach out and help. But someone who falls alone is in real trouble.

ECCLESIASTES 4:9-10

As it is, there are many parts, yet one body. The eye cannot say to the hand, "I have no need of you," nor again the head to the feet, "I have no need of you." On the contrary, the parts of the body that seem to be weaker are indispensable, and on those parts of the body that we think less honorable we bestow the greater honor, and our unpresentable parts are treated with greater modesty, which our more presentable parts do not require. But God has so composed the body, giving greater honor to the part that lacked it.

1 CORINTHIANS 12:20-24, ESV

From whom the whole body, joined and held together by every joint with which it is equipped, when each part is working properly, makes the body grow so that it builds itself up in love.

EPHESIANS 4:16, ESV

It Takes Two

I vacuum the carpet and wash the dishes at my house. What do you do in your home? Who will do what? is a question that every couple must answer. In my opinion, the gifts and abilities of each person should be considered. One may be more qualified than the other for certain tasks. Why not use the player best qualified in that area?

This does not mean that once one person accepts a responsibility, the other will never offer to help with the task. Love seeks to help and often will. In Ecclesiastes, King Solomon writes clearly about the value of teamwork. As a couple, we can accomplish more together than we can as two individuals because we are there to help each other. The Scriptures do not tell us exactly who should do what, but they do encourage us to agree on the answer.

The prophet Amos once asked, "Can two people walk together without agreeing on the direction?" (3:3). The answer is "Not very far and not very well." I encourage you to keep negotiating until both of you feel good about who is doing what in your home.

Life Promises

Iron sharpens iron, and one man sharpens another.

PROVERBS 27:17, ESV

All of you should be of one mind. Sympathize with
each other. Love each other as brothers and sisters. Be
tenderhearted, and keep a humble attitude.

1 PETER 3:8

I appeal to you, dear brothers and sisters, by the authority
of our Lord Jesus Christ, to live in harmony with each other.
Let there be no divisions in the church. Rather, be of one
mind, united in thought and purpose.

1 CORINTHIANS 1:10

The Importance of Teamwork

As a couple, what is your shared goal? Perhaps it's a smoothly running home, a harmonious relationship, and a sense of fairness. Recently, a woman was in my office complaining that her husband didn't help her with household responsibilities. "We both work full-time," she said. "But he expects me to do everything around the house while he watches TV and unwinds. Well, maybe I need to unwind too." Clearly this couple had not defined their shared goal.

The players on an athletic team do not all perform the same tasks, but they do have the same goal. That was also true when Nehemiah led the Israelites to rebuild the wall around Jerusalem. Some of them rebuilt gates, some carried materials, and others stood guard, watching for those who wanted to sabotage the work. The individuals had separate tasks, but they were united in their ultimate goal: making the city of Jerusalem safe again.

If we want harmony and intimacy in our relationship, then we must each do our part of the work. A spouse who feels put upon is not likely to be interested in intimacy. Why not ask your spouse, "Do you feel that we make a good team around the house?" Let the answer guide your actions.

Life Promises

"Don't sin by letting anger control you." Don't let the sun go down while you are still angry, for anger gives a foothold to the devil.

EPHESIANS 4:26-27

Understand this, my dear brothers and sisters: You must all be quick to listen, slow to speak, and slow to get angry. Human anger does not produce the righteousness God desires. So get rid of all the filth and evil in your lives, and humbly accept the word God has planted in your hearts, for it has the power to save your souls.

JAMES 1:19-21

People with understanding control their anger; a hot temper shows great foolishness.

PROVERBS 14:29

Just Let It Go

Do you find yourself overreacting to little irritations? Your spouse forgot the milk, and you grimace or make a sarcastic comment. Your child tracked mud on the new carpet, and you explode. If so, there is a good chance that you are suffering from stored anger—anger that has been living inside you for years.

Perhaps your parents hurt you with harsh words or severe punishment. Maybe your peers made fun of you as a teenager or your boss treated you unfairly. If you've held all these hurts inside, now your stored anger may be showing up in your behavior. The Bible wisely tells us not to let the day end when we're still angry. In other words, we need to deal with our anger right away rather than letting it build up.

Release your anger to God. Tell him about your emotions, and ask him to help you handle the situations that caused them. He can help you release the hurts from long ago and forgive those who wounded you.

Experiencing anger isn't wrong. But as Ephesians 4 tells us, letting anger control us *is* wrong—and can be very damaging to a marriage.

Life Promises

Be kind to each other, tenderhearted, forgiving one another, just as God through Christ has forgiven you.

EPHESIANS 4:32

Love your enemies! Do good to them. Lend to them without expecting to be repaid. Then your reward from heaven will be very great, and you will truly be acting as children of the Most High.

LUKE 6:35

Most important of all, continue to show deep love for each other, for love covers a multitude of sins.

1 PETER 4:8

Not So Random Acts of Kindness

"Be ye kind one to another" (Ephesians 4:32, KJV). We may have memorized it as children, but have we forgotten it as adults? Kindness is one of the traits of love, as defined in the Bible's famous "love chapter," 1 Corinthians 13: "Love is patient and kind" (v. 4). Do you consciously think of being kind to your spouse throughout the day? Kindness is expressed in the way we talk as well as in what we do. Yelling and screaming are not kind. Speaking softly and respectfully is. So is taking the time to have a meaningful conversation with a spouse who is lonely, upset, or uncertain.

Then there are acts of kindness—things we do to help others. When we focus our energy on doing kind things for each other, our relationship can be rejuvenated. What could you do today to be kind to your spouse? Maybe it's taking on a chore that's not typically your responsibility, or bringing him or her a cup of coffee in bed. Or perhaps it's giving an encouraging note or bringing home a favorite treat. These are small things, but they can have a big impact. Imagine what your relationship would be like if you both empha-sized kindness.

Life Promises

Rejoice in our confident hope. Be patient in trouble, and keep on praying.

ROMANS 12:12

Control your temper, for anger labels you a fool.

ECCLESIASTES 7:9

God blesses those who patiently endure testing and temptation. Afterward they will receive the crown of life that God has promised to those who love him.

JAMES 1:12

Patience Makes Perfect

Patience means accepting the imperfections of others. By nature, we want others to be as good as we are (or as good as we think we are), as on time as we are, or as organized as we are. The reality is, humans are not machines. The rest of the world does not live by our priority list; our agenda is not their agenda. It's especially important for couples to remember this. In a loving relationship, patience means bearing with our spouse's mistakes and giving him or her the freedom to be different from us.

When is the last time you were impatient with your significant other? Did your impatience come because he or she failed to live up to your expectations? I don't think it's coincidence that Ephesians 4:2 links humility with patience. When we're humble, we realize that the world doesn't revolve around us and that we don't set the standard for behavior. And when that's our mind-set, we're far less likely to become impatient.

The Bible says, "Love is patient and kind" (1 Corinthians 13:4). If in impatience you lash out at your loved one, love requires that you apologize and make it right. Work for more patience in your marriage.

Life Promises

Fools think their own way is right, but the wise listen to others.

PROVERBS 12:15

Come and listen to my counsel. I'll share my heart with you and make you wise.

PROVERBS 1:23

We are confident that he hears us whenever we ask for anything that pleases him. And since we know he hears us when we make our requests, we also know that he will give us what we ask for.

1 JOHN 5:14-15

Listen Up!

We will never resolve conflicts if we don't learn to listen. Many people think they are listening when in fact they are simply taking a break from talking—pausing to reload their verbal guns. Proverbs 12:15 doesn't pull any punches when it calls those who don't listen *fools*. We may not like that word, but the truth is, refusing to listen reveals a lack of humility. Wise people listen to others—especially those they love. Genuine listening means seeking to understand what the other person is thinking and feeling. It involves putting ourselves in the other person's shoes and trying to look at the world through his or her eyes.

Here's a good sentence with which to begin: "I want to understand what you are saying because I know it is important." One man told me that he made a sign which read, "I am a listener." When his wife started talking, he would hang it around his neck to remind himself of what he was doing. His wife would smile and say, "I hope it's true." He learned to be a good listener.

Life Promises

Love each other with genuine affection, and take delight in honoring each other.

ROMANS 12:10

I am praying to you because I know you will answer, O God. Bend down and listen as I pray.

PSALM 17:6

Be still, and know that I am God!

PSALM 46:10

Drop Everything!

We are all busy. Often, too busy to listen. And yet, listening is the only way we will ever come to understand our spouse's thoughts and feelings. Listening takes time and requires focus. Many people pride themselves in being able to listen while reading e-mails or watching television, but I question if that's really listening. One husband said, "My wife insists that I sit down and listen to her. I feel like I'm in a strait-jacket, like I'm wasting time."

In Romans 12, Paul tells us to "take delight in honoring each other." One way to honor someone is to listen intently and to give him or her your full attention. It's a question of respect. When you drop everything, look at your spouse, and listen, you communicate, "You are the most important person in my life." On the other hand, when you try to listen while doing other things, you communicate, "You are just one of my many interests." Listening is a powerful expression of love.

Life Promises

Some people make cutting remarks, but the words of the wise bring healing.

PROVERBS 12:18

Let everything you say be good and helpful, so that your words will be an encouragement to those who hear them.

EPHESIANS 4:29

I am certain that God, who began the good work within you, will continue his work until it is finally finished.

PHILIPPIANS 1:6

Accentuate the Positive

One of the most powerful things you can do to enhance your marriage is to choose a winning attitude. How do you do this?

First, you must admit your negative thinking. As long as you think negatively, you'll never be able to choose a winning attitude. The second step is to identify your spouse's positive characteristics, even if that's difficult for you. You might even get help from your children by asking, "What are some of the good things about Daddy or Mommy?"

Once you've identified those positive characteristics, thank God for them. Then, begin to express verbal appreciation to your spouse for the positive things you observe. Set a goal, such as giving one compliment a week for a month. Then move toward two per week, then three, and so on until you're giving a compliment each day.

The book of Proverbs has a lot to say about the importance of words. Proverbs 18:21 says, "The tongue has the power of life and death" (NIV). Proverbs 12:18 talks about words bringing healing. Proverbs 15:4 calls gentle words "a tree of life." You can give your marriage new life when you replace condemnation and criticism with compliments and words of affirmation.

Life Promises

Work willingly at whatever you do, as though you were working for the Lord rather than for people. Remember that the Lord will give you an inheritance as your reward, and that the Master you are serving is Christ.

COLOSSIANS 3:23-24

It is more blessed to give than to receive.

ACTS 20:35

Whoever wants to be first among you must be the slave of everyone else. For even the Son of Man came not to be served but to serve others and to give his life as a ransom for many.

MARK 10:44-45

Help Me Help You

The Christian message is that we serve Christ by serving others. As Colossians 3:23 says, we should do everything as if we are doing it for the Lord—in other words, willingly, cheerfully, and enthusiastically.

We all have idealistic visions of our spouse asking, "What could I do to help you tonight?" or "How could I make your life easier this week?" But the fact is, many of us grew up in homes where we had to fight to survive. We did not learn to appreciate the value of serving others. How do you develop an attitude of service if you grew up in a home where it was dog eat dog?

Let's start with your family of origin—the family you grew up in. On a scale of zero to ten, how would you rate your father on having an attitude of service toward your mother? Zero means he never lifted a finger to help her; ten means that he was almost Christlike in his servanthood. Next, rate your mother. How well did she demonstrate an attitude of service? Now let's make it personal. How would you rate yourself? Are you more like your father or your mother? Do you have a lot of room for growth? Or are you already serving Christ by serving your spouse?

Life Promises

Never let loyalty and kindness leave you! Tie them around your neck as a reminder. Write them deep within your heart.

PROVERBS 3:3

If you have a gift for showing kindness to others, do it gladly.

ROMANS 12:8

The generous will prosper; those who refresh others will themselves be refreshed.

PROVERBS 11:25

At Your Service

The theme of the Christian life is serving Christ by serving others. Jesus came to earth to serve others—first by his love, his teaching, and his healings, and ultimately by his death. When we serve others, we are not only serving Christ, but we are being Christlike. So why not begin developing an attitude of service in our closest relationship? The fact is, we do acts of service for each other every day. However, we don't often talk about them, and consequently, we begin to take them for granted.

I want to suggest a little communication exercise that will bring service to the front burner. It's a game called I Really Appreciate That. Here's how you play it: The husband might say to the wife, "One way I served you today was by putting away a load of laundry." The wife might respond, "I really appreciate that." Then she says, "One way I served you today was by cooking dinner." The husband responds, "I really appreciate that."

Play the game once a day for a week, and you will become more aware of the acts of service that you are already doing for each other. You will elevate them to a place of importance by talking about them. If you have children, let them hear you playing the game, and they'll want to get in on the fun.

Life Promises

We know what real love is because Jesus gave up his life for us. So we also ought to give up our lives for our brothers and sisters.

1 JOHN 3:16

Since God chose you to be the holy people he loves, you must clothe yourselves with tenderhearted mercy, kindness, humility, gentleness, and patience. Make allowance for each other's faults, and forgive anyone who offends you. Remember, the Lord forgave you, so you must forgive others.

COLOSSIANS 3:12-13

We love each other because he loved us first.

1 JOHN 4:19

Love Begets Love

Before my wife and I got married, I thought that every morning when the sun rises, everybody gets up. But after we were married, I found out that my wife didn't do mornings. It didn't take me long not to like her, and it didn't take her long not to like me. For several years we struggled, greatly disappointed in our marriage.

What finally turned our marriage around? The profound discovery that it was not my job to demand that she meet my expectations. My job was to give away my life to make her life easier and more meaningful. My model? Christ himself, who gave away his life for our benefit. The apostle John reminds us that Christ's sacrifice exemplifies genuine love. Because of his sacrifice, we should also give up our lives for others—starting with our spouse.

In a thousand years, I would never have come up with that idea. But then, God's ways are not our ways. In God's way of doing things, the road to greatness lies in serving others. What better place to start than in your own marriage? My wife is my first responsibility. When I choose to serve God, he says, "Let's start with your wife. Do something good for her today." When I got the picture, my wife was quick to respond. She was a fast learner.

Love begets love. That's God's way.

Life Promises

Let love be your highest goal!

1 CORINTHIANS 14:1

Above all, clothe yourselves with love, which binds us all together in perfect harmony.

COLOSSIANS 3:14

Live a life filled with love, following the example of Christ. He loved us and offered himself as a sacrifice for us.

EPHESIANS 5:2

Watch and Learn

Would you like to know your spouse's love language? Then observe how he or she most often expresses love to you. Is it through words of affirmation? gifts? acts of service? quality time? physical touch? The way a person expresses love to you is likely the way he or she wishes you would express your love.

If he often hugs and kisses you, his love language is probably *physical touch*. He wishes you would take initiative to hug and kiss him. If she is always weeding the flower beds, keeping the finances in order, or cleaning up the bathroom after you leave, then her love language is probably *acts of service*. She wishes that you would help her with the work around the house. If you don't, then she feels unloved. One husband said, "If I had known that my taking out the garbage would make her feel loved and more responsive sexually, I would have started taking out the garbage years ago." Too bad it took him so many years to learn his wife's primary love language.

As the Bible says, love should be our highest goal. To reach that goal, we need to put forth an effort to know how our spouse can best receive love.

Life Promises

God showed how much he loved us by sending his one and only Son into the world so that we might have eternal life through him. This is real love—not that we loved God, but that he loved us and sent his Son as a sacrifice to take away our sins. Dear friends, since God loved us that much, we surely ought to love each other.

1 JOHN 4:9-11

Your love for one another will prove to the world that you are my disciples.

JOHN 13:35

There is no greater love than to lay down one's life for one's friends.

JOHN 15:13

Give and You Shall Receive

I believe our deepest emotional need is the need to feel loved. If we are married, the person we most want to love us is our spouse. If we feel loved by our spouse, the whole world looks bright. If we do not feel loved, the whole world looks dark. However, we don't get love by complaining or making demands.

One man told me, "If my wife would just be a little more affectionate, then I could be responsive to her. But when she gives me no affection, I want to stay away from her." He is waiting to receive love before he gives love. Someone must take the initiative. Why must it be the other person?

Why are we so slow to understand that the initiative to love is always with us? God is our example. We love God because he first loved us. He loved us even when we were sinful, even when we weren't responsive, even when we had done nothing to deserve it. That's the ultimate example of love that takes the initiative. If you choose to give your spouse unconditional love and learn how to express love in a language your spouse can feel, there is every possibility that your spouse will reciprocate.

Life Promises

Always be humble and gentle. Be patient with each other, making allowance for each other's faults because of your love.

EPHESIANS 4:2

Do all that you can to live in peace with everyone.

ROMANS 12:18

Make every effort to keep yourselves united in the Spirit, binding yourselves together with peace.

EPHESIANS 4:3

Turn Down the Heat!

All of us have emotional hot spots. When our spouse says or does certain things, we get defensive. Usually our response is rooted in our history. You may find that often your spouse is echoing statements made by your parents that hurt or embarrassed you. The fact that you get defensive indicates that the hurt has never healed. The next time you get defensive, ask yourself why. Chances are, you will have a flood of memories. Share these past experiences with your spouse, and he or she will develop greater understanding.

What if you are the spouse? Once you learn why your husband or wife gets defensive in a certain area, then you can decide how to move on. You might ask, "How would you like me to talk about this issue in the future? I don't want to hurt you. How could I say it in a way that would not be hurtful to you?" Now you are on the road to defusing the defensive behavior of your spouse. You're also following Scripture by being patient and making allowances for your spouse's struggles, as Paul encourages in Ephesians 4:2. Learning to negotiate the "hot spots" of life is a big part of developing a growing marriage.

Life Promises

Intelligent people are always ready to learn. Their ears are open for knowledge.

PROVERBS 18:15

The heart of the godly thinks carefully before speaking.

PROVERBS 15:28

He comforts us in all our troubles so that we can comfort others. When they are troubled, we will be able to give them the same comfort God has given us.

2 CORINTHIANS 1:4

Listen and Learn

The abilities to *speak* and to *listen* are two of the more profound gifts of God. Nothing is more fundamental to a relationship than talking and listening. Open communication is the lifeblood that keeps a marriage in the spring and summer seasons—times of optimism and enjoyment. Conversely, failure to communicate is what brings on fall and winter—times of discouragement and negativity.

It sounds so simple. The problem is that many of us tend to be judgmental listeners. We evaluate what we hear based on our own view of the situation, and we respond by pronouncing our judgment. And then we wonder why our spouse doesn't talk more.

For most of us, effective listening requires a significant change of attitude. We must shift from *egocentric* listening (viewing the conversation through our own eyes) to *empathetic* listening (viewing the conversation through our partner's eyes). The goal is to discover how our spouse perceives the situation and how he or she feels. Proverbs 18:15 equates wisdom with careful listening and seeking for knowledge. In a relationship, this often means seeking knowledge about our spouse. Words are a key to the other person's heart, and listening with the intention to understand enhances conversation.

Life Promises

We don't need to write to you about the importance of loving each another, for God himself has taught you to love one another.

1 THESSALONIANS 4:9

Dear friends, let us continue to love one another, for love comes from God. Anyone who loves is a child of God and knows God. But anyone who does not love does not know God, for God is love.

1 JOHN 4:7-8

Three things will last forever—faith, hope, and love—and the greatest of these is love.

1 CORINTHIANS 13:13

Love and Be Loved

The need to love and be loved is the most fundamental of our needs. The desire to love accounts for the charitable side of humans. We feel good about ourselves when we are loving others. On the other hand, much of our behavior is motivated by the desire to *receive* love. We feel loved when we are convinced that someone genuinely cares about our well-being. The psalmist reiterates this human need to feel love in Psalm 36:7 when he thanks God for his unfailing love. The image of people taking shelter in the Lord, like chicks huddling under their mother's wings, touches us deeply because that need to be cared for is so significant.

When your spouse complains that you don't give her enough time, she is crying for love. When your spouse says, "I don't ever do anything right," he is begging for affirming words. Argue *about* the *behavior* and you will stimulate more negative behavior. Look *behind* the behavior to discover the emotional need. Meet that need, and you will eliminate the negative behavior. Love seeks to meet needs.

Life Promises

This is my commandment: Love each other in the same way I have loved you.

JOHN 15:12

Husbands ought to love their wives as they love their own bodies. For a man who loves his wife actually shows love for himself.

EPHESIANS 5:28

In the same way, you husbands must give honor to your wives. Treat your wife with understanding as you live together . . . . Be of one mind. Sympathize with each other. Love each other as brothers and sisters. Be tenderhearted, and keep a humble attitude.

1 PETER 3:7-8

Learning a New Language

What if your spouse's love language is something that doesn't come naturally for you? Maybe his love language is *physical touch*, and you're just not a toucher. Perhaps her language is *quality time*, but sitting on the couch and talking for twenty minutes is your worst nightmare.

So what are you to do?

You learn to speak your partner's language. If it doesn't come naturally for you, learning to speak it is an even greater expression of love because it shows effort and a willingness to learn. This speaks volumes to your spouse. Also, keep in mind that your love language may not come naturally for your loved one. He or she has to work just as hard to speak your language as you do to speak his or her language. That's what love is all about.

Jesus made it clear that we are to love each other as he loved us—and that is with the highest degree of sacrifice. Few of us are called to literally lay down our lives for others, but we are called to lay down our lives in small ways every day. Love is giving. Choosing to speak love in a language that is meaningful to your spouse is a great investment of your time and energy.

Life Promises

Don't be concerned for your own good but for the good of others.

1 CORINTHIANS 10:24

Jesus said to his disciples, "If any of you wants to be my follower, you must turn from your selfish ways, take up your cross, and follow me."

MATTHEW 16:24

You have been called to live in freedom, my brothers and sisters. But don't use your freedom to satisfy your sinful nature. Instead, use your freedom to serve one another in love.

GALATIANS 5:13

Love Wins

Most counselors agree that one of the greatest problems in marriage is decision making. Visions of democracy dance in the minds of many newly married couples, but when there are only two voting members, democracy often results in deadlock. How does a couple move beyond deadlock? The answer is found in one word: *love.*

Love always asks the question, What is best for you? As Paul writes in 1 Corinthians, believers need to be primarily concerned about what is beneficial for others rather than just what will help or please themselves. Love does not demand its own way. Love seeks to bring pleasure to the one loved.

That is why Christians should have less trouble making decisions than non-Christians. We are called to be lovers. When I love my wife, I will not seek to force my will upon her for selfish purposes. Rather, I will consider what is in her best interests.

Life Promises

Submit to one another out of reverence for Christ. For wives, this means submit to your husbands as to the Lord. . . . Husbands, this means love your wives, just as Christ loved the church. He gave up his life for her.

EPHESIANS 5:21-22, 25

There is one thing I want you to know: The head of every man is Christ, the head of woman is man, and the head of Christ is God.

1 CORINTHIANS 11:3

Choose today whom you will serve. . . . But as for me and my family, we will serve the LORD.

JOSHUA 24:15

Submitted for Your Approval

Many wives shudder when they hear the pastor say, "Turn in your Bible to Ephesians 5:22." They know that's the verse that says, "Wives, submit to your husbands as to the Lord" (NIV). *But you don't know my husband,* they think. I sometimes imagine that God responds, *But you don't understand submission.* Submission is not a command that applies only to females. In fact, Ephesians 5:21 instructs us to "submit to one another" because of our love for Christ.

Both the instruction to husbands about loving and the instruction to wives about submitting call for an attitude of service. Submission does not mean that the wife must do all the giving. The husband is to give his life for her. Nor does it mean that she cannot express her ideas. The goal of Paul's instructions is unity, which requires both to have an attitude of service.

Life Promises

Respect everyone, and love your Christian brothers and sisters.

1 PETER 2:17

Do to others whatever you would like them to do to you.

MATTHEW 7:12

There will be glory and honor and peace from God for all who do good.

ROMANS 2:10

Talk to Me!

I've heard many people say, "My spouse won't talk with me." If this describes your marriage, the question is, why? One reason some spouses go silent is negative communication patterns. Here are some questions to help you think about your own patterns. Consider whether you often come across as negative or complaining.

- Do I listen to my spouse when he talks, or do I cut him off and give my responses?
- Do I allow my partner space when she needs it, or do I force the issue of communication, even at those times when she needs to be alone?
- Do I maintain confidences, or do I broadcast our private conversations to others?
- Do I openly share my own needs and desires in the form of requests rather than demands?
- Do I give my spouse the freedom to have opinions that differ from my own, or am I quick to "set him straight"?

If you answer yes to the second half of any of these questions, it may be time to change your communication patterns. It's all about treating your spouse (and all believers) with respect and love, as 1 Peter 2:17 directs.

Life Promises

We are each responsible for our own conduct.

GALATIANS 6:5

If we confess our sins to him, he is faithful and just to forgive us our sins and to cleanse us from all wickedness.

1 JOHN 1:9

Knowing God leads to self-control. Self-control leads to patient endurance, and patient endurance leads to godliness.

2 PETER 1:6

Don't Play the Blame Game

Why are we so quick to blame our loved one when things aren't going well in our relationship? Unfortunately, it's human nature, going all the way back to Adam and Eve. But Galatians 6:5 reminds us that we are each responsible for our own choices and behavior, and that includes our part in a relationship.

May I suggest a better approach? Try the following steps:

1. I realize that my marriage is not what it should be.
2. I stop blaming my mate and ask God to show me where I am at fault.
3. I confess my sin and accept God's forgiveness, according to 1 John 1:9.
4. I ask God to fill me with his Spirit and give me the power to make constructive changes in my life.
5. I go to my mate, confess my failures, and ask forgiveness.
6. In God's power, I go on to change my behavior, words, and attitudes, according to the principles that I discover in Scripture.

This is God's plan, and it works. Blaming your spouse stimulates resentment and antagonism. Admitting your own failures and letting God change your behavior creates a new and positive climate in your marriage. It is the road to a growing marriage.

Life Promises

A gentle answer deflects anger, but harsh words make tempers flare.

PROVERBS 15:1

The Holy Spirit produces this kind of fruit in our lives: love, joy, peace, patience, kindness, goodness, faithfulness, gentleness, and self-control.

GALATIANS 5:22-23

Be an example to all believers in what you say, in the way you live, in your love, your faith, and your purity.

1 TIMOTHY 4:12

Be a Softy

Positive words are powerful tools in building a strong marriage. When my wife compliments me on something, it makes me want to do more. When she criticizes me, it makes me want to defend myself and fight back. If you want to see your spouse blossom, try giving a compliment every day for thirty days and see what happens.

Have you ever noticed that when you speak softly, your spouse seems to calm down, and when you speak harshly, your spouse tends to get louder? We influence each other not only by what we say, but by how we say it. Screaming is a learned behavior, and it can be unlearned. We don't have to yell at each other. Proverbs 15:1 tells us what we instinctively know: harsh words lead to more anger, but gentle words can defuse the situation. It's all in how we say it.

If you have a problem that you need to discuss with your spouse, write out what you want to say. Stand in front of a mirror and make your presentation in a soft voice. Then ask God to help you use the same tone of voice when you talk to your spouse. You may not be perfect the first time, but you will learn to speak the truth in love and gentleness.

Life Promises

Wise words satisfy like a good meal; the right words bring satisfaction. The tongue can bring death or life.

PROVERBS 18:20-21

Wise words are more valuable than much gold and many rubies.

PROVERBS 20:15

Let everything you say be good and helpful, so that your words will be an encouragement to those who hear them.

EPHESIANS 4:29

Kill Them with Kindness

This proverb is true: "The tongue can bring death or life." You can kill your spouse's spirit with negative words, and you can give life through positive words. Encouraging words should be the norm in your marriage. You can't treat encouragement like a fire extinguisher, pulling it out only when you really need it and then putting it away again. Encouragement needs to be a way of life.

Encouraging words grow out of an attitude of kindness. When I choose to be kind to my spouse, to look for her positive qualities, and to do things that will make her life easier, then positive words begin to show up in my vocabulary. Complaining, cutting remarks grow out of a negative attitude. If I focus on the worst in my spouse and think about what she should be doing for me, then I become negative. I will destroy my spouse with my negative words.

I encourage you to give your spouse life by choosing positive, affirming words. The Bible tells us that wise or helpful words bring satisfaction. Proverbs 20:15 compares the value of wise words to gold and many rubies. Encouragement can work wonders in a relationship. Look for something good in your spouse and express your appreciation. Do it today—and every day.

Life Promises

Don't use foul or abusive language.

EPHESIANS 4:29

Don't speak evil against each other, dear brothers and sisters.

JAMES 4:11

Search me, O God, and know my heart; test me and know my anxious thoughts. Point out anything in me that offends you, and lead me along the path of everlasting life.

PSALM 139:23-24

Keep It Simple

Not everyone is a born encourager, so I want to give you some practical ideas on how to increase your word power. First, *keep it simple*. Some people feel that in order to encourage, they must speak flowery words. I've sometimes called this Hallmark-itis. It's far better to use simple, straightforward words that sound like you. Your spouse will appreciate your genuine effort to express encouragement.

Second, *mean what you say*. Affirming does not mean lying or exaggerating to make your spouse feel better about himself or herself. If you're not being sincere, you'll know it and your spouse will know it, so what's the point? Better a small compliment that is sincere than a long accolade that is all fluff.

Third, *keep the focus on your spouse, not on yourself*. If your spouse tends to reflect a compliment back to you by saying, "Oh, you're far better than I in that area," gently turn the compliment back to him or her. The affirmation process is not about you but about the other person.

The Bible makes it clear that believers are to encourage one another. Ephesians 4:29 gives us a significant challenge—to let everything we say be good and helpful so that others may be encouraged. Doing so with your spouse will bring optimism and blessing to your marriage.

Life Promises

Love each other with genuine affection, and take delight in honoring each other.

ROMANS 12:10

I press on to possess that perfection for which Christ Jesus first possessed me. No, dear brothers and sisters, I have not achieved it, but I focus on this one thing: Forgetting the past and looking forward to what lies ahead, I press on to reach the end of the race and receive the heavenly prize for which God, through Christ Jesus, is calling us.

PHILIPPIANS 3:12-14

You were cleansed from your sins when you obeyed the truth, so now you must show sincere love to each other as brothers and sisters. Love each other deeply with all your heart.

1 PETER 1:22

There's No *I* in *Focus*

It has been my observation that many husbands simply do not understand the needs of their wives. Some husbands believe that if they work a steady job and bring home a decent salary, they have fulfilled their role as husband. They have little concept of a wife's emotional and social needs. Consequently, they make no effort to meet those needs.

But I have also observed that many wives do not understand their husbands' needs. Some wives believe that if they take care of the children and work with their husband to keep food on the table and keep the house in some semblance of order, they are being good wives. They have little concept of a husband's need for admiration and affection.

Often it's just a matter of focus. Why is it that when we were dating, we focused so much time and attention on each other, but after a few years of marriage, we focus on everything else? The fact is, we desperately need each other. The Bible calls us not only to love each other but to take delight in it! I want to call you to refocus attention on your spouse.

Life Promises

Look straight ahead, and fix your eyes on what lies before you. Mark out a straight path for your feet; stay on the safe path. Don't get sidetracked; keep your feet from following evil.

PROVERBS 4:25-27

Blessed are those who trust in the LORD and have made the LORD their hope and confidence. They are like trees planted along a riverbank, with roots that reach deep into the water. Such trees are not bothered by the heat or worried by long months of drought. Their leaves stay green, and they never stop producing fruit.

JEREMIAH 17:7-8

Let us hold tightly without wavering to the hope we affirm, for God can be trusted to keep his promise.

HEBREWS 10:23

Make Time for Love

Ironic, isn't it, that with all the "time savers" of modern technology, we seem to have even less time for each other? Microwaves, remote controls, dishwashers, and computers were supposed to save us valuable time. But what happened to all that extra time? Apparently, it got gobbled up by other activities. But we can reclaim some of that time for our marriages *if* we set goals and make time to reach those goals.

Proverbs 4 shows King Solomon's advice for meeting goals. Essentially, it comes down to knowing where you're going, setting a straight path to get there, and not getting sidetracked. That's the approach we need to take if we're going to meet our goals for marriage.

How do we make time? By eliminating some of the good things we are doing so that we will have time for the best. Life's meaning is not found in money, sports, shopping, academic success, or career achievement, as good as some of those things are. It is found in relationships—first with God, and then with people. If you are married, nothing is more important than your marital relationship. It is the framework in which God wants you to invest your life and experience his love. The husband is told to "love" his wife, and she is instructed to "honor" him. How better to love and honor than to make time for each other?

Life Promises

Give, and you will receive. Your gift will return to you in full—pressed down, shaken together to make room for more, running over, and poured into your lap. The amount you give will determine the amount you get back.

LUKE 6:38

It is more blessed to give than to receive.

ACTS 20:35

Give generously, for your gifts will return to you later.

ECCLESIASTES 11:1, TLB

Little Things Mean a Lot

When is the last time you gave your spouse a gift? What did you give? If you can't answer those questions, a gift is long overdue. Gift giving is one of the five fundamental languages of love. A gift to your spouse is visible evidence of your loving thoughts.

The most famous gifts in the Bible are undoubtedly the gifts from the wise men to the baby Jesus. These men brought costly gifts of gold and expensive spices, and in doing so they honored Jesus and showed that they believed him to be a king. I'm sure Mary and Joseph were awed by these beautiful things and the love for their son these gifts signified.

The gift need not be expensive. Guys, you can get flowers free. Just go out in your yard and pick one. That's what your children do. No flowers in your yard? Try your neighbors' yard. Ask them; they'll give you a flower.

However, if you can afford to buy gifts, don't give free flowers. Why not invest some of your money in your marriage? Give your spouse something you know will be appreciated. If you're not certain, ask! Explain that you want to do something nice, and ask for a list of some things your spouse would like to have. That's valuable information. Use it to build your relationship.

Life Promises

You must have the same attitude that Christ Jesus had.
Though he was God, he did not think of equality with
God as something to cling to. Instead, he gave up his divine
privileges; he took the humble position of a slave and was
born as a human being. When he appeared in human
form, he humbled himself in obedience to God and died
a criminal's death on a cross.

PHILIPPIANS 2:5-8

Always be full of joy in the Lord. . . . Don't worry about
anything; instead, pray about everything. Tell God what you
need, and thank him for all he has done.

PHILIPPIANS 4:4, 6

Faith is the confidence that what we hope for will actually
happen; it gives us assurance about things we cannot see.

HEBREWS 11:1

It's All about Attitude

How does your relationship with God affect your marriage? Profoundly!

By nature, I'm self-centered. I carry that attitude into my marriage. So when I don't get my way, I argue or sulk. That doesn't lead to a growing marriage. My attitude must change, and that's where God comes into the picture. He is in the business of changing attitudes.

The apostle Paul says, "You must have the same attitude that Christ Jesus had." What was his attitude? He was willing to step from heaven to earth to identify with us—something that one translation describes as "becoming nothing." Once he became a man, he was willing to step down even further and die for us. Jesus' attitude is first and foremost an attitude of sacrificial love and service. If that attitude is in me, I will have a growing marriage.

My research has shown that not a single wife in the history of this nation has ever murdered her husband while he was washing the dishes. Not one! That's a bit tongue-in-cheek, but it ought to tell us something.

Developing this attitude of service may seem impossible, but it's not. Never underestimate God's power to transform a willing individual.

Life Promises

If you abide in My word, you are My disciples indeed. And you shall know the truth, and the truth shall make you free.

JOHN 8:31-32, NKJV

I pray that from his glorious, unlimited resources he will empower you with inner strength through his Spirit. Then Christ will make his home in your hearts as you trust in him.

EPHESIANS 3:16-17

I can do all things through Christ who strengthens me.

PHILIPPIANS 4:13, NKJV

Eliminate the Negative

The way you perceive yourself greatly affects your marriage. Some people grow up thinking of themselves as failures. This perception keeps them in bondage. Their attitude is, *Why try? I'll fail anyway.* When these people fall in love and get married, they bring this distorted self-perception into the marriage.

I can tell you that such a person's spouse will be greatly frustrated. Often, someone who thinks of himself or herself as a failure will expect a spouse to build him or her up, but it doesn't take long for the spouse to discover that such efforts are futile.

If you recognize yourself as having a distorted self-perception, please realize that your spouse cannot change the way you see yourself. Only you can do that.

So where do you start? In John 8, Jesus says that the truth will make you free—free from sin, and free from wrong patterns of thinking. What is the truth about you, according to God's Word? You are made in God's image, highly valued by him, and especially gifted to serve in his Kingdom.

Believe the truth about yourself. Discover your abilities, and give them to God. He will make you a success. When you do this, you will free your spouse from having to battle the way you view yourself—and you will free yourself from negative thinking.

Life Promises

Don't copy the behavior and customs of this world, but let God transform you into a new person by changing the way you think.

ROMANS 12:2

Be an example to all believers in what you say, in the way you live, in your love, your faith, and your purity.

1 TIMOTHY 4:12

In everything we do, we show that we are true ministers of God.

2 CORINTHIANS 6:4

It's Never Too Late to Change

How would you describe yourself? How would you describe your spouse? Are you optimistic or pessimistic? Critical or complimentary? Is your spouse extroverted or introverted? Patient or impatient? The way you perceive yourself and the way you perceive your spouse will make a difference in your behavior and, consequently, in your marriage.

Unfortunately, we have been led to believe these traits are set in concrete by the age of five or six and that we cannot change them. The good news is that we don't have to be controlled by these perceptions. The message of the Bible is that we *can* change, with God's help. Romans 12:2 makes clear that if we're willing, God will transform us. He can change us at a heart level by altering the very way we think.

If you perceive yourself as being negative and critical, practice the art of giving compliments. You might begin by giving *yourself* a compliment. Find something you did well, then stop long enough to say, "Hey, I did a good job with that." If you give yourself one compliment every day, before long you will change your self-perception. Do the same for your spouse, and watch him or her begin to live up to your compliments too.

You can change your self-perceptions—and the way you interact with your spouse—for the better.

Life Promises

God decided in advance to adopt us into his own family by bringing us to himself through Jesus Christ. This is what he wanted to do, and it gave him great pleasure. . . . And when you believed in Christ, he identified you as his own by giving you the Holy Spirit, whom he promised long ago.

EPHESIANS 1:5, 13

Two people are better off than one, for they can help each other succeed. . . . Three are even better, for a triple-braided cord is not easily broken.

ECCLESIASTES 4:9, 12

Think of ways to motivate one another to acts of love and good works.

HEBREWS 10:24

T-E-A-M

It seems to me that if we could understand God better, we could understand marriage better. Ever notice how God the Father, God the Son, and God the Holy Spirit work together as a team? Read the first chapter of Ephesians and observe how the Father planned our salvation, the Son shed his blood to effect our salvation, and the Holy Spirit sealed our salvation. God is one within the mystery of the Trinity, and this unity is expressed in the diversity of roles needed to accomplish one goal, our salvation.

The Scriptures say that, in marriage, the husband and wife are to become one flesh. However, this unity does not mean that we are clones of each other. No, we are two distinct creatures who work together as a team to accomplish one goal—God's will for our lives. In mundane things such as washing clothes and mopping floors, or in exciting things such as volunteering in a soup kitchen or leading a Bible study, we complement each other. The husband who takes care of the children while his wife leads a Bible study is sharing with her in ministry. Indeed, two become one when they work together as a team.

Life Promises

[Jesus] began to wash the disciples' feet, drying them with the towel he had around him. . . . [He said,] "Since I, your Lord and Teacher, have washed your feet, you ought to wash each other's feet. I have given you an example to follow. Do as I have done to you."

JOHN 13:5, 14-15

Encourage those who are timid. Take tender care of those who are weak. Be patient with everyone.

1 THESSALONIANS 5:14

God has given each of you a gift from his great variety of spiritual gifts. Use them well to serve one another.

1 PETER 4:10

The Hallmark of a Great Marriage

In every vocation, those who excel are those who have a genuine desire to serve others. The most notable physicians view their vocation as a calling to serve the sick and diseased. Truly great politicians see themselves as "public servants." The greatest of all educators seeks to help students reach their full potential.

It is no different in the family. A great husband is a man who views his role as helping his wife accomplish her objectives. And a great wife is a woman who gives herself to helping her husband succeed. In giving their lives to each other, they both become winners.

Holding on to your rights and demanding that your spouse serve you is exactly the opposite of what the Bible teaches. The Scriptures say, "Give, and you will receive" (Luke 6:38), not "Demand, and people will do what you demand." The fact is, most people do not respond well to demands—but few people will reject loving service. Service follows the example of Jesus and is the hallmark of greatness.

Life Promises

Marriage should be honored by all, and the marriage bed kept pure.

HEBREWS 13:4, NIV

Husbands, love your wives, as Christ loved the church and gave himself up for her, that he might sanctify her, having cleansed her by the washing of water with the word, so that he might present the church to himself in splendor, without spot or wrinkle or any such thing, that she might be holy and without blemish. In the same way husbands should love their wives as their own bodies. He who loves his wife loves himself. For no one ever hated his own flesh, but nourishes and cherishes it, just as Christ does the church.

EPHESIANS 5:25-29, ESV

Those who belong to Christ Jesus have nailed the passions and desires of their sinful nature to his cross and crucified them there.

GALATIANS 5:24

2=1

The book of Genesis says that when a husband and wife have sexual intercourse, they become "one flesh" (Genesis 2:24, NIV). In other words, their two lives are bonded together. Sex is the consummating act of marriage. We have a public wedding ceremony and a private consummation of the public commitment. Sexual intercourse is the physical expression of the inward union of two lives.

In the ancient Hebrew Scriptures and in the New Testament writings, sexual intercourse is always assumed to be reserved for marriage. That is not an arbitrary denunciation of sex outside of marriage but simply an effort to be true to the nature of sexual intercourse. Such deep bonding is inappropriate outside a loving, lifetime commitment between a husband and a wife. The author of the book of Hebrews talks about keeping the marriage bed pure—in other words, keeping sexual intercourse as a special thing only between a husband and wife.

Sex is not simply a matter of joining two bodies that were uniquely made for each other. It touches on intellectual, emotional, social, and spiritual bonding as well. Sex was God's idea, and marriage is the context in which it finds ultimate meaning.

Life Promises

Give your burdens to the LORD, and he will take care of you.
He will not permit the godly to slip and fall.

PSALM 55:22

Don't worry about anything; instead, pray about everything.
Tell God what you need, and thank him for all he has done.
Then you will experience God's peace, which exceeds
anything we can understand. . . . Fix your thoughts on what
is true, and honorable, and right, and pure, and lovely,
and admirable. Think about things that are excellent and
worthy of praise.

PHILIPPIANS 4:6-8

Commit everything you do to the LORD. Trust him, and he
will help you.

PSALM 37:5

The 4:8 Principle

Trying to keep a positive attitude is not a new idea. It is found clearly in the first-century writing of Paul the apostle. He encouraged the church at Philippi to pray about problems rather than worry about them. Why? Because worry leads to anxiety and negativity, while prayer leads to peace and a more positive outlook. Then Paul revealed the key to having a positive attitude: think about positive things—things that are "excellent and worthy of praise."

We are responsible for the way we think. Even in the worst marital situation, we choose our attitude. Maintaining a positive attitude requires prayer. As Paul said, we can bring our requests to God. We can tell him what we need and be thankful for what he has already done. Will God always do what we ask? No, but what does happen is that as we release worry and express gratitude, God's peace descends on our minds and hearts. God calms our emotions and directs our thoughts.

When we find ourselves struggling with an aspect of our marriage, let's try to develop a more optimistic perspective. With a positive attitude, we become a part of the solution, rather than a part of the problem.

Life Promises

I pray for you constantly, asking God, the glorious Father of our Lord Jesus Christ, to give you spiritual wisdom and insight so that you might grow in your knowledge of God.

EPHESIANS 1:16-17

I tell you, you can pray for anything, and if you believe that you've received it, it will be yours.

MARK 11:24

We are confident that he hears us whenever we ask for anything that pleases him. And since we know he hears us when we make our requests, we also know that he will give us what we ask for.

1 JOHN 5:14-15

The Couple That Prays Together

Martin Luther said, "As it is the business of tailors to make clothes and cobblers to mend shoes, so it is the business of Christians to pray." Intercession is one ministry that requires no special spiritual gift. All Christians are equipped to pray.

Not only is intercessory prayer a ministry, it is also a responsibility. The prophet Samuel told the Israelites, "I will certainly not sin against the LORD by ending my prayers for you" (1 Samuel 12:23). The apostle Paul began many of his epistles by telling his readers how frequently he prayed for them. Prayer is one of the means that God has chosen to let us cooperate with him in getting his work done. It is a ministry that husbands and wives can do together. They can pray for each other as well as for their children, their parents, their pastor and church, other ministries, and world missions.

If you don't have a daily prayer time with your spouse, why not start today? Ask your spouse to spend five minutes praying with you. If you don't want to pray out loud, then pray silently. Take the first step in learning the ministry of intercessory prayer.

Life Promises

Wise words satisfy like a good meal; the right words bring satisfaction. The tongue can bring death or life.

PROVERBS 18:20-21

All of you should be of one mind. Sympathize with each other. Love each other as brothers and sisters. Be tenderhearted, and keep a humble attitude.

1 PETER 3:8

So then, let us aim for harmony . . . and try to build each other up.

ROMANS 14:19

You Said It!

First Corinthians 8:1 says, "Love edifies" (NKJV) or "builds up" (NIV). So if I want to love, I will use words that build up my spouse. "You look nice in that outfit." "Thanks for taking the garbage out." "I loved the meal. Thanks for all your hard work." "I appreciate your walking the dog for me Tuesday night. It was a real help." All of these are expressions of love.

Proverbs 18:21 tells us, "Death and life are in the power of the tongue" (NKJV). Words are powerful. You can kill your spouse's spirit with negative words—words that belittle, disrespect, or embarrass. You can give life with positive words—words that encourage, affirm, or strengthen. I met a woman some time ago who complained that she couldn't think of anything good to say about her husband. I asked, "Does he ever take a shower?" "Yes," she replied. "Then I'd start there," I said. "There are men who don't."

I've never met a person about whom you couldn't find something good to say. And when you say it, something inside the person wants to be better. Say something kind and life giving to your spouse today and see what happens.

Life Promises

Dear children, let's not merely say that we love each other;
let us show the truth by our actions.

1 JOHN 3:18

Love is patient and kind. Love is not jealous or boastful or
proud or rude. It does not demand its own way. It is not
irritable, and it keeps no record of being wronged. It does
not rejoice about injustice but rejoices whenever the truth
wins out. Love never gives up, never loses faith, is always
hopeful, and endures through every circumstance.

1 CORINTHIANS 13:4-7

This is my commandment: Love each other in the same way
I have loved you.

JOHN 15:12

Just Do It!

The apostle John writes in 1 John 3:18 that we should show our love for each other through actions, not just words. It can be easy to speak words, but our sincerity is proved through what we do. *Do* something to show your love.

Love is kind, the Bible says (1 Corinthians 13:4). So to express your love, find something kind and do it. It might be giving him an unexpected gift, or washing the car that he drives. It might be offering to stay home with the children while she goes shopping or hiking. Or perhaps it's picking up dinner on the way home when you know she's had a hectic day. How long has it been since you wrote your spouse a love letter?

Love is patient (1 Corinthians 13:4). So stop pacing the floor while your spouse is getting ready to go. Sit down, relax, read your Bible, and pray. Love is also courteous. The word means "courtlike." So do some of the things you did when you were courting. Reach over and touch his knee or take her hand. Open the door for her. Say please and thank you. Be polite. Express your love by your actions.

Life Promises

The body is a unit, though it is made up of many parts; and though all its parts are many, they form one body. So it is with Christ.

1 CORINTHIANS 12:12, NIV

Live in harmony and peace. Then the God of love and peace will be with you.

2 CORINTHIANS 13:11

Make allowance for each other's faults, and forgive anyone who offends you. Remember, the Lord forgave you, so you must forgive others.

COLOSSIANS 3:13

Reconcilable Differences

What are some of the differences between you and your spouse? If you are an optimist, your spouse may be a pessimist. Often, one spouse is quiet; the other is talkative. One tends to be organized with everything in its place; the other spends half a lifetime looking for car keys.

After years of arguing about differences, couples often conclude that they are incompatible. In fact, incompatibility—or "irreconcilable differences"—is often cited as the grounds for divorce. However, after thirty years of counseling married couples, I'm convinced that there are no irreconcilable differences, only people who refuse to reconcile.

In God's mind, our differences are designed to be complementary, not to cause conflicts. The principle is illustrated by the church, as the apostle Paul describes in 1 Corinthians 12. Each member performs a different role, yet each is seen as an important part of the body. Believers can accomplish far more when we function as a team. Why can't we get this working in our marriages? It all begins by accepting our differences as an asset rather than a liability. Why not begin by thanking God that you and your spouse aren't exactly alike?

Life Promises

I want [believers] to be encouraged and knit together by strong ties of love.

COLOSSIANS 2:2

May God, who gives this patience and encouragement, help you live in complete harmony with each other, as is fitting for followers of Christ Jesus.

ROMANS 15:5

Gentle words are a tree of life.

PROVERBS 15:4

Can We Talk?

The Scriptures indicate that husbands and wives are to become "one." They are to share life to such a degree that they have a sense of unity, or togetherness. The apostle Paul states his vision for believers: that they would be "knit together" or "united in love" (Colossians 2:2, NIV). This is critical for all believers and even more so for marriage partners.

Would you describe your marriage like this?

- "We are a team."
- "We know each other."
- "We understand each other."
- "We choose to walk in step with each other."
- "Our lives are inseparably bound together."
- "We are one."

These are the statements of happily married couples. Such togetherness does not happen without a lot of communication. Communication is a two-way street. I talk and you listen; you talk and I listen. It is this simple process that develops understanding and togetherness.

How much time do you spend in conversation with your spouse each day? Perhaps it's time to think about establishing a daily sharing time.

Life Promises

Be still, and know that I am God; I will be exalted among the nations, I will be exalted in the earth.

PSALM 46:10, NIV

As the deer longs for streams of water, so I long for you, O God. I thirst for God, the living God. When can I go and stand before him?

PSALM 42:1-2

Draw near to God and He will draw near to you.

JAMES 4:8, NKJV

Us Time

After the creation of Adam and Eve, God said that the two should become one. Becoming "one" does not mean that we lose our personal identities. We retain our personalities, and we still have personal goals and ambitions. We each have our own pursuits; the typical husband and wife spend many hours each day geographically separated from each other. Marital "oneness" is not sameness. It is rather that inner feeling that assures us that we are "together" even when we are apart.

Many couples have found that the secret to growing in oneness is establishing a daily sharing time. Many people have a daily "quiet time" with God for the purpose of getting close to him. As the author of Psalm 42 conveys so beautifully, when we're strong in our relationship with God, we long for him and desire to be near him. The same thing can be true with our spouse. The more we set aside time to spend together, the more important it becomes to us.

I encourage you to consider having a daily sharing time with your spouse for the purpose of staying close to each other. Set aside time each day to talk and to share your thoughts, emotions, and concerns. Conversation leads to understanding and unity.

Life Promises

The LORD himself watches over you! The LORD stands beside you as your protective shade. The sun will not harm you by day, nor the moon at night.

PSALM 121:5-6

O LORD, you have searched me and you know me. You know when I sit and when I rise; you perceive my thoughts from afar.

PSALM 139:1-2, NIV

Plant the good seeds of righteousness, and you will harvest a crop of love.

HOSEA 10:12

Three Things

Psalm 139 makes clear that God knows our every thought and even our words before we speak them. The Lord knows us—effortlessly—better than we know ourselves. But it takes effort for a man and woman to know each other. Do you see then why communication is an absolute necessity if we are to understand our spouse?

We cannot know our spouse's thoughts, feelings, or desires unless he or she chooses to tell us and we choose to listen. That is why a daily sharing time is so important in a marriage. We cannot develop a sense of "togetherness" unless we talk regularly with each other.

A daily sharing time is a time set aside each day for the purpose of talking and listening. If you're unsure what to talk about, try this: "Tell me three things that happened in your life today and how you feel about them." It can start with ten minutes and may extend to thirty or longer. The key is not the length but the consistency. I have never seen a truly successful marriage that did not *make* time for communication.

Life Promises

Better a dry crust eaten in peace than a house filled with feasting—and conflict.

PROVERBS 17:1

A servant of the Lord must not quarrel but must be kind to everyone, be able to teach, and be patient with difficult people. Gently instruct those who oppose the truth.

2 TIMOTHY 2:24-25

God blesses those who work for peace, for they will be called the children of God.

MATTHEW 5:9

Surprise—People Are Human!

Do you ever feel like you are married to an alien? Early in your relationship you thought you were so compatible. In fact, you agreed on everything. Now perhaps you wonder how you ever got together, because you are so different. Welcome to the world of reality. The fact is, you are married to a human. Humans don't all think the same way and don't all feel the same way. In short, all human relationships include conflicts. The key is to learn constructive methods for reaching resolution when a conflict arises.

For starters, never discuss disagreements "on the run." Rather, set aside time specifically for resolving conflict. Once a week, have a "conflict resolution session." The rest of the week, try to focus on the things you like about each other. Make positive comments about your spouse. This creates a healthy climate in which to discuss your conflicts.

When you set aside time to deal with conflict, you avoid having your house continually filled with angry words or frustration—a situation King Solomon clearly found unpalatable, based on Proverbs 17:1. When you allow room for peace, you will work through your conflicts one by one without destroying your relationship. Every resolved conflict brings you and your loved one closer together.

Life Promises

Share each other's burdens, and in this way obey the law of Christ.

GALATIANS 6:2

Confess your sins to one another and pray for one another, that you may be healed.

JAMES 5:16, ESV

Where two or three are gathered in my name, there am I among them.

MATTHEW 18:20, ESV

Tell Me about It

Most of the couples I meet wish that they could share more freely with each other about their spiritual journeys. We often speak of emotional intimacy or sexual intimacy with our spouse, but we seldom talk about spiritual intimacy. Yet this affects all other areas of our relationship.

Just as emotional intimacy comes from sharing our feelings, spiritual intimacy comes from sharing about our walks with God. We don't have to be spiritual giants to have spiritual intimacy as a couple, but we must be willing to share with each other where we are spiritually.

The husband who says, "I'm not feeling very close to God today" may not stimulate great joy in his wife's heart, but he does open the possibility for her to enter into his spiritual experience. If she responds with, "Tell me about it," she encourages spiritual intimacy. If, however, she says, "Well, if you don't feel close to God, guess who moved?" she has stopped the flow, and he walks away feeling condemned.

The apostle Paul challenges us to share each other's burdens, and those often include feelings of spiritual dryness or difficulty. Spiritual intimacy within a marriage requires a willingness to listen without preaching.

Life Promises

When we get together, I want to encourage you in your faith, but I also want to be encouraged by yours.

ROMANS 1:12

Her husband can trust her, and she will greatly enrich his life. She brings him good, not harm, all the days of her life.

PROVERBS 31:11-12

You husbands must give honor to your wives. Treat your wife with understanding as you live together. . . . She is your equal partner in God's gift of new life.

1 PETER 3:7

God Talk

One wife said to me, "I wish that my husband and I could share more about spiritual things. He seems willing to talk about everything else, but when I mention church, God, or the Bible, he clams up and walks away. I don't know what to do, but it's very frustrating." What advice would you give this wife?

Here's what I said: "Don't ever stop talking about spiritual things. Your relationship with God is the most important part of your life. If you don't share this part of yourself, your husband will never know who you are. However, don't expect him to reciprocate, and don't preach him a sermon until he asks for one. Simply share what God is doing in your life. Share a Scripture that helped you make a decision or encouraged you when you were feeling down.

"When you share what your spiritual life is like, you stimulate hunger. When your husband gets spiritually hungry, he will likely want to discuss things with you. At that point, spiritual intimacy will begin."

Encouraging each other in our faith is a valuable goal. Even the apostle Paul wanted to be encouraged by seeing the faith of the Roman believers. When we reach the point of sharing our spiritual successes and struggles, our marriage will be blessed.

Life Promises

"You will seek me and find me when you seek me with all
your heart. I will be found by you," declares the LORD.

JEREMIAH 29:13-14, NIV

Come and listen to my counsel. I'll share my heart with you
and make you wise.

PROVERBS 1:23

Know this, my beloved brothers: let every person be quick
to hear, slow to speak, slow to anger.

JAMES 1:19, ESV

Stop. Look. Listen.

What are the rewards of listening to your spouse? Listening is the doorway into your spouse's heart and mind. God told Israel, "I know the plans I have for you. . . . They are plans for good and not for disaster, to give you a future and a hope" (Jeremiah 29:11). But how was Israel to know what was on God's heart and in God's mind? Verses 13 and 14 make it clear that they would discover the Lord when they sought him wholeheartedly. God wanted Israel to know his thoughts, but Israel had to listen.

What are you doing to seek to know the thoughts and feelings of your spouse? Listening is the key to good communication. Don't condemn your spouse for not talking more. Rather, ask questions, and then listen to the answers. They may be short at first, especially if your spouse is not the talkative type. But once your spouse realizes that you are truly interested, she will eventually share her thoughts. Accept your spouse's thoughts as interesting, challenging, or fascinating, and he will talk more.

Listening to God brings you close to his heart. Listening to your spouse brings you the same kind of intimacy.

Life Promises

Who can find a virtuous and capable wife? She is more precious than rubies. Her husband can trust her, and she will greatly enrich his life. She brings him good, not harm, all the days of her life. . . . When she speaks, her words are wise, and she gives instructions with kindness.

PROVERBS 31:10-12, 26

Let the one who has never sinned throw the first stone!

JOHN 8:7

When God our Savior revealed his kindness and love, he saved us, not because of the righteous things we had done, but because of his mercy.

TITUS 3:4-5

Get with the Program

What's a wife to do when her husband refuses to "get with the program"? You have asked him again and again to change. You've told him exactly what you want, but he doesn't budge. So what are you to do?

Let me suggest that you take a different approach. Start with yourself. Look carefully at your own behavior and ask yourself, *What have I been doing that I should not be doing? What have I been saying that I should not be saying?*

Then, confess these things to God and then to your husband. Even if your husband is 95 percent of the problem, the place for you to start is with your 5 percent. After all, you *can* change that, and when you do, your marriage will be 5 percent better.

Consider this approach from a wife who tends to treat her husband like hired help: "It was unfair of me to ask you to get rid of that tree stump right after you mowed the lawn. I know I've piled tasks on you before, and I'm sorry. I want you to know that I appreciate the work you did this morning." Whatever his initial response, she has just changed the climate of her marriage.

Strive to be a wife who, like the famous "Proverbs 31 woman," speaks wisely and kindly, and brings good to her husband.

Life Promises

Love each other with genuine affection, and take delight in honoring each other.

ROMANS 12:10

Let your wife be a fountain of blessing for you. Rejoice in the wife of your youth. She is a loving deer, a graceful doe. . . . May you always be captivated by her love.

PROVERBS 5:18-19

His mouth is sweetness itself; he is desirable in every way. Such, O women of Jerusalem, is my lover, my friend.

SONG OF SONGS 5:16

Delight in Each Other

The desire for romantic love is deeply rooted in our psychological makeup. Almost every popular magazine has at least one article on keeping love alive. So why is it that so few couples seem to have found the secret to a lasting love *after* the wedding? I'm convinced it's because we concentrate on *getting* love rather than *giving* love.

As long as you focus on what your spouse should be doing for you, you'll come across as condemning and critical. How about a different approach—one that says, "What can I do to help *you*? How can I make *your* life easier? How can I be a better spouse?" In Romans 12, Paul writes that when we love each other, we should "take delight in honoring each other." Giving to the one we love does not have to be a chore; if our affection is genuine, giving and serving can be a joy. *Giving* love will keep your relationship alive.

Life Promises

Whenever we have the opportunity, we should do good to everyone—especially to those in the family of faith.

GALATIANS 6:10

Let your light shine before others, so that they may see your good works and give glory to your Father who is in heaven.

MATTHEW 5:16, ESV

Someone will say, "You have faith and I have works." Show me your faith apart from your works, and I will show you my faith by my works.

JAMES 2:18, ESV

At Your Service

For some people, actions speak louder than words. Acts of service is probably the primary love language of these people. It's what makes them feel loved. The words *I love you* may seem shallow to these folks if they are not accompanied by acts of service.

Mowing the grass, cooking a meal, washing dishes, vacuuming the floor, getting hairs out of the sink, removing the white spots from the mirror, getting bugs off the windshield, taking out the garbage, changing the baby's diaper, painting the bedroom, dusting the bookcase, washing the car, trimming the shrubs, raking the leaves, dusting the blinds, walking the dog—these types of things communicate love to the person whose primary love language is acts of service. In Galatians, Paul encourages us to take opportunities to do good and kind things for other believers. How much more should we do this for the one we love most?

Do these things, and your spouse will feel loved. Fail to do these things, and you can say, "I love you" all day long without making him or her feel loved. If you want your spouse to feel loved, you must discover and speak his or her primary love language.

Life Promises

Let everything you say be good and helpful, so that your words will be an encouragement to those who hear them.

EPHESIANS 4:29

Do not deprive one another, except perhaps by agreement for a limited time, that you may devote yourselves to prayer.

1 CORINTHIANS 7:5, ESV

Therefore a man shall leave his father and his mother and hold fast to his wife, and they shall become one flesh.

GENESIS 2:24, ESV

Pillow Talk

If there is one skill that is more important than any other in gaining sexual oneness, it is *communication*. Why are we so ready to discuss everything else and so reticent to communicate openly about this area of marriage? When talking about sexuality, we should endeavor to follow the apostle Paul's advice and share helpful, encouraging words with each other. Your communication can make a dramatic difference to the level of mutual sexual satisfaction in your marriage.

Your wife will never know your feelings, needs, and desires if you do not express them. Your husband will never know what pleases you if you do not communicate. I have never known a couple who gained mutual sexual satisfaction without open communication about sexual matters. You cannot work on a problem of which you are unaware.

Let me share a practical idea to help you get started. At the top of a sheet of paper, write these words: "These are things I wish my spouse would do or not do to make the sexual part of our marriage better for me." Write down some ideas, and then share your lists with each other. Information opens the road to growth. Remember, your goal is making sex a mutual joy.

Life Promises

Let me see your face; let me hear your voice. For your voice is pleasant, and your face is lovely.

SONG OF SONGS 2:14

Give honor to marriage, and remain faithful to one another in marriage.

HEBREWS 13:4

There are many virtuous and capable women in the world, but you surpass them all!

PROVERBS 31:29

The Joy of Sex

Why is sex such an important part of marriage? We are sexual creatures by God's design. The most obvious purpose of sexuality is reproduction, but that is not the only one.

A second purpose is companionship. God said of Adam, "It is not good for the man to be alone" (Genesis 2:18). God's answer was the creation of Eve and the institution of marriage, about which Scripture says, "The two are united into one" (Genesis 2:24). That's true literally and metaphorically. In sexual intercourse, we bond with each other. It is the opposite of being alone. It is deep intimacy, deep companionship.

A third purpose of sex is pleasure. Song of Songs is replete with illustrations of the pleasure of relating to each other sexually within marriage. The descriptive phrases may be foreign to our culture (an American man wouldn't typically compare his wife's teeth to sheep, for example), but the intent is clear: maleness and femaleness are meant to be enjoyed by marriage partners.

Sex was not designed to be placed on the shelf after the first few years of marriage. God's desire is that we find and enjoy mutual sexual love throughout our married life.

Life Promises

You husbands must give honor to your wives. Treat your wife with understanding as you live together.

1 PETER 3:7

Do not deprive one another, except perhaps by agreement for a limited time, that you may devote yourselves to prayer.

1 CORINTHIANS 7:5, ESV

Drink water from your own well—share your love only with your wife.

PROVERBS 5:15

Love and Be Loved

When the word *intimacy* is mentioned, many husbands immediately think of sex. But sex cannot be separated from intellectual and emotional intimacy. The failure to recognize this reality leads to marital frustration.

If a woman does not feel free to express her ideas, or if she feels that her husband does not respect her ideas and will tell her they're foolish if she shares them, then she may have little interest in being sexually intimate with him. Her feelings of condemnation and rejection make it difficult for her to be sexually responsive.

If a wife does not feel loved by her husband, again the emotional distance stands as a barrier to sexual intimacy. A husband who ignores these realities will be frustrated by his wife's lack of interest in sex. The problem is not her lack of interest. Rather, it is the emotional barriers that exist between the two of them.

The apostle Peter encourages men to honor their wives and treat them with understanding and consideration. Men should do this first and foremost because God commanded it, but the truth is that it benefits them as well. The wise husband will seek to create a climate where his wife feels accepted and loved as a person. In doing so, he opens the door to sexual intimacy.

Life Promises

Each man must love his wife as he loves himself, and the wife must respect her husband.

EPHESIANS 5:33

The heart of the godly thinks carefully before speaking; the mouth of the wicked overflows with evil words.

PROVERBS 15:28

I will give them singleness of heart and put a new spirit within them. I will take away their stony, stubborn heart and give them a tender, responsive heart.

EZEKIEL 11:19

Is Anyone Listening?

Most of us share our ideas much too soon. We talk before we have really listened. In fact, one research project found that the average person will listen only seventeen seconds before interrupting.

Good listeners will never share their ideas until they are sure that they understand what the other person is saying. In marriage, this is extremely important. Ask questions, repeat what you think your spouse is saying, and ask, "Am I understanding you?" When your spouse says, "Yes, I think you understand what I'm saying and how I feel," then and only then are you ready to move on. You might say, "I really appreciate your being open with me. Now that I understand where you're coming from, may I share what I was thinking when I did that? I realize now that what I said was hurtful, but I want you to understand that I was not trying to hurt you."

At this point, your spouse will hear your perspective, because you have first taken the time to really hear what he or she was saying.

Life Promises

Teach us to realize the brevity of life, so that we may grow in wisdom.

PSALM 90:12

Seek first the kingdom of God and his righteousness, and all these things will be added to you.

MATTHEW 6:33, ESV

Do not be conformed to this world, but be transformed by the renewal of your mind, that by testing you may discern what is the will of God, what is good and acceptable and perfect.

ROMANS 12:2, ESV

The Oughts

Have you heard people say, "I know that I ought to, but I just don't have time"? Is it true that we don't have time to do what we ought to do? The word *ought* means to be bound by moral law, conscience, or a sense of duty. If we are not accomplishing our *oughts*, then we need to examine our use of time.

Time is a resource the Lord has given us, and like any other resource, we need to be good stewards of it. Psalm 90:12, and many other verses in the Bible, underscores the bottom-line reason for using our time well—because our time on earth is limited. Time is a precious commodity we shouldn't waste.

Ultimately, we can control how we use our time. We can accomplish our goals for our closest relationships. Making time for what's important means that we must say no to things of lesser importance. Do you need to sit down and take a fresh look at how you are using your time? Then do it today.

Life Promises

Dear children, let's not merely say that we love each other; let us show the truth by our actions.

1 JOHN 3:18

We know that God causes everything to work together for the good of those who love God and are called according to his purpose for them.

ROMANS 8:28

Keep on asking, and you will receive what you ask for. Keep on seeking, and you will find. Keep on knocking, and the door will be opened to you. For everyone who asks, receives. Everyone who seeks, finds. And to everyone who knocks, the door will be opened.

MATTHEW 7:7-8

Extending Love's Life Span

Falling in love is a temporary experience. It is not premeditated; it simply happens in the normal context of male-female relationships. What many people do not know is that it is always temporary. The average life span for being "in love" is two years.

The "in love" experience temporarily meets our emotional need for love. It gives us the feeling that someone cares, that someone admires and appreciates us. Our emotions soar with the thought that another person sees us as number one. For a brief time our emotional need for love is met. However, when we come down off the emotional high, we may feel empty. That's sometimes accompanied by feelings of hurt, disappointment, or anger.

The apostle John recounted an important truth when he wrote his first epistle: love can be expressed in words, but it is shown to be true through our actions. Learn the language of your spouse, speak it regularly, and emotional love will return to your marriage.

Life Promises

May the Lord lead your hearts into a full understanding and expression of the love of God and the patient endurance that comes from Christ.

2 THESSALONIANS 3:5

Let's not get tired of doing what is good. At just the right time we will reap a harvest of blessing if we don't give up.

GALATIANS 6:9

God is working in you, giving you the desire and the power to do what pleases him.

PHILIPPIANS 2:13

A Daily Dose

One husband said to his wife, "You know I love you. Why do I have to keep saying it?" Another said, "I gave you a gift for your birthday. That was only two months ago. What do you mean I don't ever give you anything?"

Both of these husbands failed to realize that expressions of love must become a normal way of life, not occasional acts.

Emotional love must be nurtured. Speaking the primary love language of your spouse is the best way to keep love alive. So if *acts of service* is your spouse's love language, then cook a meal, clean the house, or mow the grass, and watch his or her love tank fill. If it's *words of affirmation*, give her a compliment, and she will feel loved. If it's *quality time*, sit on the couch and give him your undivided attention. If it's *physical touch*, put your hand on her shoulder. If it's *gifts*, give him a book, card, or special treat.

Love is a choice you make daily. As you make that choice, as the passage from 2 Thessalonians 3:5 says, the Lord will lead you into a greater understanding and expression of his love. He will teach you to love like he does.

Life Promises

Don't copy the behavior and customs of this world, but let God transform you into a new person by changing the way you think. Then you will learn to know God's will for you, which is good and pleasing and perfect.

ROMANS 12:2

Hope in the LORD; for with the LORD there is unfailing love. His redemption overflows.

PSALM 130:7

I pray that God, the source of hope, will fill you completely with joy and peace because you trust in him. Then you will overflow with confident hope through the power of the Holy Spirit.

ROMANS 15:13

There Is Hope!

A husband recently said to me, "I don't know what else to do. I find my love feelings for my wife dying and being replaced by pity and anger. I want to respect her. I want to love her. I want to help her, but I don't know how." Thousands can identify with the constant frustration of living with a difficult or irresponsible spouse.

Is there hope? Yes, and it begins with you. You must first of all adopt a positive attitude. This husband is doing what most of us do by nature: he is focusing on the problem rather than on the solution. There are scores of steps he can take, but they require a positive attitude.

First, he must agree that God is still in the business of changing lives. Romans 12:2 reminds us that God can transform us from the inside out. If we turn to God, he can change our thinking, which in turn will change our patterns of acting. There is hope. This husband must pray, "Father, I know there is an answer to our problems. Please show me the next step." This focus on seeking solutions will lead him to answers.

Life Promises

The earnest prayer of a righteous person has great power and produces wonderful results.

JAMES 5:16

Be truly glad. There is wonderful joy ahead, even though you have to endure many trials for a little while.

1 PETER 1:6

Let us hold tightly without wavering to the hope we affirm, for God can be trusted to keep his promise.

HEBREWS 10:23

Praying for Change

True or false? When you are in a bad marriage, there are only two options: resign yourself to a life of misery, or get out.

Many couples live in deep pain. They have tried to improve things and have failed. Thus, they accept the commonly held dichotomy: I need to get out and start over, or else I must accept the fact that I'm going to live in misery the rest of my life.

I want to suggest that there is a third option: let God use you as a positive change agent in your marriage. You can't make your spouse change. However, you can positively influence your spouse to change. Most of us underestimate the power of influence.

We also underestimate the power of prayer. The Scriptures include many examples of people pleading with God—and his answering them. James 5:16 tells us that our earnest prayer can bring remarkable results. And the apostle Paul reminds believers to devote themselves to prayer and to pray constantly in Colossians 4. So pray for your relationship. Ask God to give you a clear picture of how you got to where you are in your marriage. Ask him to show you how you might be an instrument in his hand to influence your spouse. It's a prayer he will answer. And he will give you the power to do it.

Life Promises

Against you, and you alone, have I sinned; I have done what is evil in your sight. You will be proved right in what you say, and your judgment against me is just. . . . Purify me from my sins, and I will be clean; wash me, and I will be whiter than snow.

PSALM 51:4, 7

Whenever you stand praying, forgive, if you have anything against anyone, so that your Father also who is in heaven may forgive you your trespasses.

MARK 11:25, ESV

Judge not, and you will not be judged; condemn not, and you will not be condemned; forgive, and you will be forgiven.

LUKE 6:37, ESV

Forgiveness

I wish that I were a perfect husband: always kind, thoughtful, understanding, considerate, and loving. Unfortunately, I am not. None of us are. I am sometimes selfish, thoughtless, and cold. In short, I fail to live up to the biblical ideal for a Christian husband. Does that mean that my marriage is destined for failure? Not if I am willing to admit my failures and if my wife is willing to forgive.

Forgiveness does not mean simply overlooking or ignoring the other person's failures. God's forgiveness should be our model. God forgives us based on what Christ did for us on the cross. God does not overlook sin, and God does not forgive everyone indiscriminately. God forgives *when* we confess our sin and express our need for forgiveness. Psalm 51, written by King David after his sin of adultery with Bathsheba, is a helpful model of true remorse for wrongdoing. David admitted his guilt, acknowledged God's justice, and asked for God's purifying forgiveness. And God gave it to him.

Genuine confession always precedes true forgiveness. So in order to have a growing marriage, I must confess my failures to my wife, and she must forgive me.

Life Promises

Give all your worries and cares to God, for he cares about you.

1 PETER 5:7

Repay no one evil for evil, but give thought to do what is honorable in the sight of all.

ROMANS 12:17, ESV

If you forgive others their trespasses, your heavenly Father will also forgive you.

MATTHEW 6:14, ESV

Forgive and Forget?

There is a difference between forgiving and forgetting. One wife said, "I've forgiven him, but I have trouble with my feelings when I remember what he did." Forgiveness does not destroy our memory. Our brains record every event we have ever experienced, good and bad. Memory may bring back the event and the feelings of hurt and pain. But keep in mind that forgiveness is not a feeling. Rather, it is a promise to no longer hold the sin against the other person.

So what do we do when the memory comes back and we feel the pain? We take it to God and say, "Father, you know what I'm remembering, and you know the pain I'm feeling, but I thank you that it is forgiven. Now help me to do something loving for my spouse today." We don't allow the memory to control our behavior. In time, the pain will diminish as we build new positive memories together. Don't be troubled by memories. As 1 Peter 5:7 reminds us, we can bring all our worries to God. He cares about us and will help us forgive.

Life Promises

Sensible people control their temper; they earn respect by overlooking wrongs.

PROVERBS 19:11

His anger lasts only a moment, but his favor lasts a lifetime! Weeping may last through the night, but joy comes with the morning.

PSALM 30:5

Don't sin by letting anger control you. Think about it overnight and remain silent.

PSALM 4:4

Where Did That Come From?

If you seem to have lost the spark in your marriage, if your enthusiasm for life is waning, or if you find yourself irritable and often snap at your spouse or children, you may be suffering from long-term anger.

When we overreact to little irritations, it is a sign that we have anger stored inside. Stored anger can eventually lead to huge explosions. That's when people wonder, *What happened to him?* because the explosion seems out of character. But what people have not seen is the buildup of anger that has been going on inside the person, perhaps for years.

When we hold anger inside instead of getting rid of it, the pressure mounts. In Proverbs 14:13, King Solomon wisely observes that hidden emotions don't just go away. That's why the Bible says, "Don't let the sun go down while you are still angry" (Ephesians 4:26). Get rid of anger quickly. If you don't, you can become a chronically angry person, ready to explode at any time. That's never good for your marriage.

Life Promises

We know how much God loves us, and we have put our trust in his love. God is love, and all who live in love live in God, and God lives in them.

1 JOHN 4:16

God so loved the world, that he gave his only Son, that whoever believes in him should not perish but have eternal life.

JOHN 3:16, ESV

Keep loving one another earnestly, since love covers a multitude of sins.

1 PETER 4:8, ESV

All You Need Is Love

I really do believe that "love makes the world go round."
Why would I say that? Because God is love. It is his love for
us that makes all of life meaningful. First John 4 reminds us
that when we realize how much God loves us, it is so mag-
nificent that we put our trust in that love. Even those who
do not believe in God are the recipients of his love. He gives
them life and the opportunity to respond to his love. He
wants to forgive and enrich their lives. His plans for them
are good.

What does all of this have to do with marriage? God
instituted marriage because he loved us. His intention was
certainly not to make us miserable; he made us for each
other. Husband and wife are designed to work together as
a mutually supportive team to discover and fulfill God's
plans for their lives. It's beautiful when it works.

What is the key to having that kind of marriage? In a
word, *love.* It is the choice to look out for each other in the
same way that God looks out for us. It is allowing God to
express his love through us. It doesn't require warm feelings,
but it does require an open heart.

Life Promises

Such love has no fear, because perfect love expels all fear.

1 JOHN 4:18

I can do everything through Christ, who gives me strength.

PHILIPPIANS 4:13

I am convinced that nothing can ever separate us from God's love. Neither death nor life, neither angels nor demons, neither our fears for today nor our worries about tomorrow—not even the powers of hell can separate us from God's love.

ROMANS 8:38

The Power of Love

Love is not our only emotional need, but it interfaces with all our other needs. We also need to feel secure, to have a healthy sense of self-worth, and to feel that our lives are significant.

The apostle John writes, "Perfect love casts out fear" (1 John 4:18, NKJV). In our relationship with God, this means that when we know the Lord loves us and has saved us, we are no longer afraid of judgment. In a sense, we can face anything. Genuine love in a human relationship has some of the same effects. Why should I be afraid if I am loved?

If I feel loved by my wife, then I also feel good about myself. After all, if she loves me, I must be worth loving. Ultimately, it is discovering that God loves me that gives me my greatest sense of worth. But my wife is an agent of God's love.

If my spouse loves me, I'm also more likely to feel that my life has significance. We want our lives to count for something; we want to make a difference in the world. When we give love to and receive love from our spouse, we *are* making a difference. We are enriching his or her life. This is what God called us to do—express his love in the world.

Life Promises

Let us think of ways to motivate one another to acts of love and good works.

HEBREWS 10:24

Everything else is worthless when compared with the infinite value of knowing Christ Jesus my Lord. For his sake I have discarded everything else, counting it all as garbage, so that I could gain Christ and become one with him.

PHILIPPIANS 3:8-9

He who finds a wife finds a good thing and obtains favor from the LORD.

PROVERBS 18:22, ESV

Two Are Better Than One

Marriage gives a husband and wife an opportunity to minister to each other. They accept each other as they are, but they can also encourage each other to excellence. God has plans for each life. Spouses can help each other succeed in accomplishing these plans, and often this is done by expressing love.

Not everyone feels significant. Some people grew up in homes where they were given negative messages: *You are not smart enough. You're not athletic or talented. You'll never amount to anything.* All of these messages are false, but if they are all you have ever heard, you are likely to believe them.

When you learn your spouse's primary love language and speak it regularly, you are filling his love tank. You are also impacting her concept of herself. *If he loves me,* she thinks, *I must be significant.* You become God's agent for helping your spouse feel loved. Few things are more important in encouraging your spouse to accomplish God's plans. As the author of Hebrews writes, as believers, we should consider how we can encourage each other to greater love and service. That's even more true within a marriage.

Marriage is designed to help us accomplish more for God. Two are better than one in his Kingdom.

Life Promises

An open rebuke is better than hidden love! Wounds from a sincere friend are better than many kisses from an enemy.

PROVERBS 27:5-6

Rejoice in hope, be patient in tribulation, be constant in prayer.

ROMANS 12:12, ESV

Be still before the LORD and wait patiently for him; fret not yourself over the one who prospers in his way, over the man who carries out evil devices! Refrain from anger, and forsake wrath! Fret not yourself; it tends only to evil. For the evildoers shall be cut off, but those who wait for the LORD shall inherit the land.

PSALM 37:7-9, ESV

Never Stop

If you're like most couples, you will arrive at a point in your relationship (likely multiple points) where, instead of sharing your feelings and trying to resolve differences, you will be tempted to ask yourself, *Why bother?* Don't make that mistake. Once communication lines are down between you and your spouse, it may be difficult to restore them.

Maintaining communication with your spouse will take a boatload of patience and persistence. At times, you may feel like you're beating your head against a wall. Take some aspirin, and keep pounding. Eventually, your work will pay off.

Never assume that silence or indifference is preferable to conflict. It's not. Proverbs 27:5 makes it clear: sincerity is always better than buried feelings. Truthful responses can be painful, but they can also bring healing and genuine communication. As long as you and your spouse are interacting and actively trying to resolve your differences, there's hope. When you stop talking, hope dies. Keep your relationship on the front burner. Neglect your relationship, and you will poison your intimacy. Talking and listening are the ways we learn to work together as a team, and that's what a growing marriage is all about.

Life Promises

Oh, the joys of those who . . . delight in the law of the LORD, meditating on it day and night. They are like trees planted along the riverbank, bearing fruit each season. Their leaves never wither, and they prosper in all they do.

PSALM 1:1-3

Commit your actions to the LORD, and your plans will succeed.

PROVERBS 16:3

We are God's masterpiece. He has created us anew in Christ Jesus, so we can do the good things he planned for us long ago.

EPHESIANS 2:10

It's a Wonderful Life

What is success? Ask a dozen people, and you may get a dozen different answers. A friend of mine said, "Success is making the most of who you are with what you've got." I like that definition. Every person has the potential to make a positive impact on the world.

Psalm 1 compares a successful person to a tree—planted by the riverbank, stable and with deep roots, healthy, flourishing, and fruitful. When we are deeply rooted in God, he can use us and we can make a significant difference in the world. It all depends on what we do with what we have. Success is not measured by the amount of money we possess or the position we attain, but by how we use our resources and our opportunities. Position and money can be used to help others, or they can be squandered or abused. Truly successful people are those who help others succeed.

The same is true in marriage. A successful wife is one who expends her time and energy helping her husband reach his potential for God and for doing good in the world. Likewise, a successful husband is one who helps his wife do the same. If you help your spouse succeed, you end up living with a winner—and someone who feels fulfilled and purposeful. Not a bad life.

Life Promises

[Love] does not demand its own way.

1 CORINTHIANS 13:5

The husband should fulfill his wife's sexual needs, and the wife should fulfill her husband's needs. The wife gives authority over her body to her husband, and the husband gives authority over his body to his wife. Do not deprive each other of sexual relations.

1 CORINTHIANS 7:3-5

Don't look out only for your own interests, but take an interest in others, too.

PHILIPPIANS 2:4

Making Love

How are you doing in meeting your spouse's sexual needs? In 1 Corinthians 7, husbands and wives are challenged to meet each other's sexual needs. "Do not deprive each other," the Scripture says. Our bodies are to be a gift to each other; we are to be available to give sexual pleasure to each other. This is God's design.

Why do we often struggle so much to experience this mutual pleasure? Perhaps we have forgotten the key ingredient of love. Love means looking out for the other person's interests. The question is, how may I bring you pleasure? Love doesn't demand its own way. Love is not pushy or irritable, but thinks first of how to please the other person.

It's sad that "Let's make love" has often been reduced to "Let's have sex." Sex without genuine loving care for each other will be empty indeed. God's idea is that sex will be an expression of our deep love and lifelong commitment to each other. Anything short of this misses God's intention.

Life Promises

Our earthly fathers disciplined us for a few years, doing the best they knew how. But God's discipline is always good for us, so that we might share in his holiness.

HEBREWS 12:10

Let all that you do be done in love.

1 CORINTHIANS 16:14, ESV

Love is patient and kind; love does not envy or boast; it is not arrogant or rude. It does not insist on its own way; it is not irritable or resentful; it does not rejoice at wrongdoing, but rejoices with the truth. Love bears all things, believes all things, hopes all things, endures all things. Love never ends.

1 CORINTHIANS 13:4-8, ESV

Love Is . . .

"I did it because I love her." We often use the word *love* to explain our behavior. Who doesn't remember a parent saying, "I'm punishing you because I love you"? As children we had a hard time figuring that out, but it was likely true. Parents discipline children because they love them.

But in a marriage, there is no parent—only two partners. We don't discipline each other, but we do love each other and want our partner to fulfill his or her God-given potential.

The question is, how do we know when our actions are loving? Love is doing what is best for the other person, but at times this can be difficult to figure out. For example, the wife of an alcoholic picks up the pieces after her husband's latest episode. She calls it love, but the psychologist calls it codependency. Did her action help him? Perhaps in the short term, but not in the long term.

We must learn to love effectively by doing what will best serve the emotional, spiritual, and physical health of our spouse. At times that means love must be tough. If this is a situation you face, ask God to give you the wisdom to make the right choices about how best to love your spouse.

Life Promises

Take delight in the LORD, and he will give you your heart's desires. Commit everything you do to the LORD. Trust him, and he will help you.

PSALM 37:4-5

Fix your thoughts on what is true, and honorable, and right, and pure, and lovely, and admirable. Think about things that are excellent and worthy of praise. Keep putting into practice all you learned and received from me—everything you heard from me and saw me doing. Then the God of peace will be with you.

PHILIPPIANS 4:8-9

[Love] does not demand its own way.

1 CORINTHIANS 13:5

Taking the Intimidation out of Intimacy

What is the biblical picture of intimacy in marriage? It's found in Genesis 2:25: "The man and his wife were both naked, but they felt no shame." This is a vivid image of marital intimacy: two distinct persons, equal in value, totally transparent, and without fear of being known. It is that kind of openness, acceptance, trust, and excitement to which we refer when we use the word *intimacy*.

But this was before sin entered the picture. It's interesting that Adam and Eve's immediate response to eating the forbidden fruit was to feel shame at their nakedness and cover themselves. In other words, after sin there were clothes. Something came between Adam and Eve, and they were no longer transparent. They were no longer willing to be freely known; now they had to work at intimacy.

The same is true for us. Because we are fallen creatures, we sometimes fear being known. Why? Because with intimacy comes the possibility of condemnation and rejection. To overcome that fear, we must develop a relationship of trust with our spouse.

Life Promises

We ask God to give you complete knowledge of his will and to give you spiritual wisdom and understanding.

COLOSSIANS 1:9

Don't worry about anything; instead, pray about everything. Tell God what you need, and thank him for all he has done. Then you will experience God's peace, which exceeds anything we can understand. His peace will guard your hearts and minds as you live in Christ Jesus.

PHILIPPIANS 4:6-7

If you remain in me and my words remain in you, you may ask for anything you want, and it will be granted!

JOHN 15:7

And Now, God, about My Spouse . . .

Praying for your spouse may be your greatest ministry. What could be more important? Through word and example, the Bible shows us that prayer is powerful. James 5:16 says, "The earnest prayer of a righteous person has great power and produces wonderful results."

Daniel fasted and prayed in great humility, confessing his sins and the sins of Israel. Paul prayed that the Christians at Colosse would be filled with the knowledge of God's will. Jesus prayed that Peter's faith would not fail after he denied Christ.

How are you praying for your spouse? Perhaps you could use Colossians 1:9-14 as a place to begin. As you pray for your spouse what Paul prayed for these believers—that their faith would be strengthened and that God would equip them with endurance and patience—you will be ministering to him or her. You may also find your heart growing more tender toward your spouse.

Prayer is one of God's ordained means of accomplishing his will on earth. As he allows us to preach and teach, so he allows us to pray—and so we cooperate with him in his work. Pray for your spouse today, and watch how it affects your marriage.

Life Promises

[Jesus said,] "Where two or three gather together as my followers, I am there among them."

MATTHEW 18:20

Pray in the Spirit at all times and on every occasion. Stay alert and be persistent in your prayers for all believers everywhere.

EPHESIANS 6:18

The LORD is close to all who call on him, yes, to all who call on him in truth.

PSALM 145:18

Just Close Your Eyes and Pray

Many couples find it difficult to pray together. Why? One reason may be that they are not treating each other with love and respect, and that stands as a barrier between them. The answer to this problem is confession and repentance. First John 1:9 says, "If we confess our sins to him, he is faithful and just to forgive us our sins." It is a sin to fail to love your spouse, or to fail to treat him or her with kindness and respect. Such sin needs to be confessed and forgiven; then the couple will be able to pray together.

A second reason couples are unable to pray together may be that one or both of them have never learned to pray with another person. To many people, prayer is private. While you should pray in private *for* your spouse, you should also pray *with* your spouse. After all, Jesus told his disciples that if even two or three of them were gathered together, he would be present among them. That's a powerful statement and a great testimony to praying together as a couple.

An easy way to get started is with silent prayer. It works like this: you hold hands, close your eyes, and then pray silently. When you have finished praying, you say, "Amen," and then wait until your spouse says, "Amen." Praying silently while holding hands is one way of praying together, and it will enhance your marriage.

Life Promises

Respect everyone, and love your Christian brothers and sisters.

1 PETER 2:17

Two people are better off than one, for they can help each other succeed. If one person falls, the other can reach out and help. But someone who falls alone is in real trouble.

ECCLESIASTES 4:9-10

Make every effort to keep yourselves united in the Spirit, binding yourselves together with peace. For there is one body and one Spirit, just as you have been called to one glorious hope for the future.

EPHESIANS 4:3-4

I Love You—Please Change!

If you're newly married, you may have discovered some things about your loved one that you're not crazy about. He snores like a lumberjack. She squeezes the toothpaste in the middle. He clips his toenails in front of the TV and leaves the evidence on the coffee table. She sings the wrong lyrics to every song on the radio.

The key to working through such irritations is to keep them in their proper perspective. Don't let small things become big problems. Remind yourself that these are not life-threatening issues. If you can find solutions, fine. If not, you can live with them.

Try this: tell your spouse three things you like about him or her, and then make one request. For example, "Could you please rinse the hairs out of the sink when you finish getting ready in the morning?" Since commendation preceded your request, your spouse is more likely to accept the request for change.

One guideline: never request change more than once every two weeks. Perhaps you could agree that this week your spouse may make a request of you, and next week you can request a change. The bottom line is respect. The apostle Peter encourages us to treat each other with love and respect, and that certainly applies to our spouse. When you are polite, loving, and respectful, you will see changes happen.

Life Promises

Let's not get tired of doing what is good. At just the right time we will reap a harvest of blessing if we don't give up.

GALATIANS 6:9

The generous will prosper; those who refresh others will themselves be refreshed.

PROVERBS 11:25

To those who use well what they are given, even more will be given, and they will have an abundance. But from those who do nothing, even what little they have will be taken away.

MATTHEW 25:29

I Do. Now What?

Too many couples view the wedding as the finish line of their relationship. They work and work to make it to their wedding day, and then they sit back and wait for "happily ever after" to begin.

That's not how marriage works. If doing nothing is your strategy for keeping love alive in your relationship, you're in trouble. It's similar to Christians who see salvation as the final step in the journey. Once that's done, they think they can coast spiritually for the rest of their lives. But that's hardly biblical.

Paul encourages us to persist in service and good deeds. We need to keep working on our relationship with God, and we also need to keep working on our marriage relationship. Remember, the wedding is the first step, not the final one. To make your relationship work over the long haul, you need to invest the same kind of time, energy, and effort after the wedding as you invested when you were dating.

What were some of the things you did when you were dating? Did you give gifts? Did you go to nice restaurants? Did you open the car door for her? Maybe it's time to ask your spouse, "Of all the things I did when we were dating, which would you most like for me to do now?" Let his or her answer lead you to a growing marriage.

Life Promises

We know how dearly God loves us, because he has given us the Holy Spirit to fill our hearts with his love.

ROMANS 5:5

This is real love—not that we loved God, but that he loved us and sent his Son as a sacrifice to take away our sins.

1 JOHN 4:10

Don't just pretend to love others. Really love them. Hate what is wrong. Hold tightly to what is good. Love each other with genuine affection, and take delight in honoring each other.

ROMANS 12:9-10

Unconditional Love

How can we love an unlovely spouse? Through more than thirty years of counseling, I have met with many individuals who live in unbelievably difficult marriages. Without exception, the root problem of marital difficulties is selfishness, and the root cure is love. Love and selfishness are opposites. By nature we are all self-centered, but when we become Christians, the Holy Spirit brings the love of God into our hearts, as Romans 5:5 indicates. Galatians 5:22-23 lists the character qualities the Holy Spirit will produce in our lives if we allow him, and these include love. We now can become God's agents for expressing his love. Sharing this divine love flowing through us is the most powerful thing we can do for our spouse.

I want to give you the challenge I have given many people through the years. Try a six-month experiment of loving your spouse unconditionally. Discover your spouse's primary love language, and speak it at least once a week for six months, no matter how you are treated in return. I have seen hard, harsh, cruel people melt long before the six months are over. When you let God express his love through you, you can become the agent of healing for your spouse and your marriage.

Life Promises

Worry weighs a person down; an encouraging word cheers a person up.

PROVERBS 12:25

I will give you a new heart, and I will put a new spirit in you. I will take out your stony, stubborn heart and give you a tender, responsive heart.

EZEKIEL 36:26

We love each other because he loved us first.

1 JOHN 4:19

A Kind Word Goes a Long Way

Many couples have never learned the tremendous power of verbally affirming each other. Verbal compliments, or words of affirmation, are powerful communicators of love. King Solomon, author of the ancient Hebrew wisdom literature we find in the Bible, wrote several proverbs about words. Proverbs 12:25 highlights the importance of encouraging words. Proverbs 18:21 is even more dramatic, saying, "The tongue can bring death or life." Cutting, critical comments can kill a person's spirit, but affirming words bring renewal and hope.

Read the following statements and ask yourself, *Have I said anything similar to my spouse within the last week?*

· "You look sharp in that outfit."
· "Wow! Do you ever look nice in that dress!"
· "You have got to be the best potato cook in the world. I love these potatoes."
· "Thanks for getting the babysitter lined up tonight. I want you to know I don't take that for granted."
· "I really appreciate your washing the dishes."
· "I'm proud of you for getting that positive job review. You're a hard worker, and it shows."

Want to improve your marriage? Say something positive to your spouse today.

Life Promises

I am leaving you with a gift—peace of mind and heart. And the peace I give is a gift the world cannot give. So don't be troubled or afraid.

JOHN 14:27

This means that anyone who belongs to Christ has become a new person. The old life is gone; a new life has begun!

2 CORINTHIANS 5:17

I pray that God, the source of hope, will fill you completely with joy and peace because you trust in him. Then you will overflow with confident hope through the power of the Holy Spirit.

ROMANS 15:13

Marriage Myths

I want to share four myths that often destroy our motivation for working on our marriages. If I believe these myths, I will be in bondage, but the walls of my prison will really be made of paper. They can only hold me if I think they're too strong for me to break through. Jesus told his hearers that when we know the truth, it will set us free. We can be free from these myths when we counter them with truth.

Myth #1: *My state of mind and the quality of my marriage are determined by my environment.*
The Truth: God can give peace of mind even in the worst of situations (see John 14:27). I can be God's instrument for improving my marriage.

Myth #2: *People cannot change.*
The Truth: People do change every day, often dramatically. God is in the business of changing lives (see 2 Corinthians 5:17).

Myth #3: *When you are in a bad marriage, you have only two options: be miserable or get out.*
The Truth: You can be a positive change agent in your marriage (see Romans 12:2).

Myth #4: *Some situations are hopeless.*
The Truth: With God, no situation is hopeless (see Romans 15:13). He is the God of miracles. Focus your eyes on him rather than on your situation.

Life Promises

Do not judge, or you too will be judged. For in the same way you judge others, you will be judged, and with the measure you use, it will be measured to you. Why do you look at the speck of sawdust in your brother's eye and pay no attention to the plank in your own eye? . . . First take the plank out of your own eye, and then you will see clearly to remove the speck from your brother's eye.

MATTHEW 7:1-3, 5, NIV

Does anyone want to live a life that is long and prosperous? Then keep your tongue from speaking evil and your lips from telling lies!

PSALM 34:12-13

Since God chose you to be the holy people he loves, you must clothe yourselves with tenderhearted mercy, kindness, humility, gentleness, and patience. Make allowance for each other's faults, and forgive anyone who offends you. Remember, the Lord forgave you, so you must forgive others. Above all, clothe yourselves with love, which binds us all together in perfect harmony. And let the peace that comes from Christ rule in your hearts. For as members of one body you are called to live in peace. And always be thankful.

COLOSSIANS 3:12-15

Pot, Meet Kettle

It is easy for us to identify the failures of our mates, but more difficult to admit our own. When couples come to me for counseling, I often give both individuals a sheet of paper and ask them to list their spouse's faults. They will write profusely for ten or fifteen minutes. Some even ask for more paper.

Then I ask them to make a list of their own faults. Most people can think of *one*. But I have seen them sit there and sit there trying to think of a second. Seldom has anyone come up with more than four things on that list. We see twenty-seven things wrong with our spouse, but we only have four on our own list.

We tend to see ourselves through rose-colored glasses. Our faults do not look very big to us because we are used to them. Naturally, then, we attribute the real problem to our mate's behavior. But Jesus warned us not to judge each other, because the level of criticism we use against others will be used against us—likely by our spouse! He tells us to first get the plank out of our own eye. Once we've done that, we can see more clearly to help our mate deal with his or her faults.

Life Promises

A new command I give you: Love one another. As I have loved you, so you must love one another.

JOHN 13:34, NIV

The LORD is slow to anger and filled with unfailing love, forgiving every kind of sin and rebellion.

NUMBERS 14:18

The LORD will withhold no good thing from those who do what is right.

PSALM 84:11

Look a Little Deeper

We will never be able to address the real problems in a relationship until we understand what motivates the other person's behavior. All of our behavior is motivated by inner needs, including the need for love.

Barb complains that her husband doesn't have time for her. She often raises her voice and delivers angry lectures to him, accusing him of not caring for her. Sometimes these lectures work, and her husband, Bob, will sit down and talk with her—but he is typically resentful. How much better their interactions would be if Bob understood that Barb's primary love language is quality time and made an effort to talk with her regularly. Addressing her need for love might well eliminate her negative behavior.

As believers, we're called to love each other as Christ loves us. That was the "new command" Jesus gave his disciples in John 13, and it's a tall order. But one way we can go about that is to make sure we're responding patiently, even when provoked. Loving our spouse with Christlike love means looking at his or her heart. Learning to identify the emotional need that is behind your spouse's behavior—rather than just arguing about the symptoms—is a major step in being a positive influence in an otherwise difficult relationship. Don't curse the behavior. Address the need.

Life Promises

The LORD has declared today that you are his people, his own special treasure, just as he promised.

DEUTERONOMY 26:18

Seek the Kingdom of God above all else, and live righteously, and he will give you everything you need.

MATTHEW 6:33

Set your minds on things that are above, not on things that are on earth.

COLOSSIANS 3:2, ESV

All Work, No Play?

Is your spouse a workaholic? If so, you need to understand that the desire for significance is one of the primary emotional needs that push some people. Many workaholics do not realize that our real significance comes from being children of God and living out his plans for us. After all, Deuteronomy 26 talks about God's children as his own "special treasure." Our heavenly Father loves us not because of anything we are or do, but because he created us. We can't do anything to increase or decrease our value in his sight.

Workaholics tend to forget this. As a result, they put all their effort into excelling in the marketplace and often neglect even their closest relationships. Perhaps a man's father said, "You will never amount to anything"—so he spends a lifetime trying to prove his father wrong. It's a bitter, never-ending cycle.

If you are married to a workaholic, don't curse your spouse's work. Instead, offer praise, admiration, and encouragement. Say how proud you are. The more praise you give, and the more you value your spouse for who he or she is rather than for what he or she does, the more likely your workaholic partner will be to spend more time away from work and with you.

Life Promises

God so loved the world, that he gave his only Son, that whoever believes in him should not perish but have eternal life.

JOHN 3:16, ESV

If I speak in the tongues of men and of angels, but have not love, I am a noisy gong or a clanging cymbal. And if I have prophetic powers, and understand all mysteries and all knowledge, and if I have all faith, so as to remove mountains, but have not love, I am nothing. If I give away all I have, and if I deliver up my body to be burned, but have not love, I gain nothing.

1 CORINTHIANS 13:1-3, ESV

Anyone who loves another brother or sister is living in the light.

1 JOHN 2:10

Unconditional Love

When you got married, did you sign a contract or make a covenant? When you sign a mortgage contract, the bank loans you the money *if* you agree to make the monthly payments. Stop making payments, and the bank will foreclose on your house to get its money back.

Many couples have the same attitude about marriage. They might say, "I will love you and be faithful to you *if* you will love me and be faithful to me." That is not the biblical view of marriage. Biblically, marriage is a covenant, not a contract. Covenant marriage is based on unconditional love—love no matter what.

God is the author of unconditional love. Romans 5:8 reminds us that God loved us and sacrificed for us even when we were sinful, undeserving, and ungrateful. The prophet Isaiah even compared our best efforts to "filthy rags" (64:6). We have nothing to offer God, but he loves us nonetheless. Loving the unlovely is the hallmark of God. It is also the key to a successful marriage.

Life Promises

When I refused to confess my sin, my body wasted away, and I groaned all day long. . . . Finally, I confessed all my sins to you and stopped trying to hide my guilt. I said to myself, "I will confess my rebellion to the LORD." And you forgave me! All my guilt is gone.

PSALM 32:3, 5

If you forgive those who sin against you, your heavenly Father will forgive you.

MATTHEW 6:14

Look at those who are honest and good, for a wonderful future awaits those who love peace.

PSALM 37:37

Love Means Never Having to Say, "I'm Sorry."

The classic seventies movie *Love Story* advised us that true love means never having to say, "I'm sorry." I don't think they got it right, for one simple reason: we are all human, and humans are not perfect. All of us end up hurting the people we love most. Having a good marriage does not demand perfection, but it does require us to apologize when we fail.

When I say, "I'm sorry," I'm expressing regret that my words or behavior have brought you pain. It's a basic guideline for getting along with others. It also reflects the spiritual truth that to receive forgiveness, we first need to admit what we've done. Ignoring our sin doesn't make it go away, as King David experienced before he wrote the words of Psalm 32. In fact, ignoring it often makes us feel far worse. But when we express regret for our wrongdoing and the hurt it caused, we pave the way for forgiveness and reconciliation. That's true in our relationship with God as well as in our marriage.

When is the last time you said, "I'm sorry," to your husband or wife? If it's been awhile, then you probably owe him or her an apology. Love means always being willing to say, "I'm sorry."

Life Promises

The ear tests the words it hears just as the mouth distinguishes between foods.

JOB 12:11

Be kind to one another, tenderhearted, forgiving one another, as God in Christ forgave you.

EPHESIANS 4:32, ESV

Trust in the LORD with all your heart, and do not lean on your own understanding.

PROVERBS 3:5, ESV

Saying vs. Doing

Perhaps you have said, "I'm sorry," but your spouse is finding it hard to forgive you. You may feel frustrated and say to yourself, *I apologized. What else can I do?* If you're serious, I'll tell you. Ask your spouse this question: "What can I do to make this up to you?" You might also say, "I know I hurt you, and I feel bad about it, but I want to make it right. I want to do something to show you that I love you."

This is far more powerful than simply saying, "I'm sorry." Why? Because sometimes words don't mean much unless they're backed up with action. The Old Testament figure Job was overrun with words from his friends, who tried to make sense of his terrible suffering. But much of what they said was wrong, and in chapter 12, Job says that he tested their words to determine what was true. We all do the same thing—test words to see if they are genuine and if they will likely be followed up with action.

To establish trust, you need to show that your words are genuine. When you ask your spouse how you can make the situation right, you are trying to make restitution. You are demonstrating that you really care about your relationship. After all, what your spouse wants to know is whether your apology is sincere. Make sure your answer is clear.

Life Promises

The purpose of my instruction is that all believers would be filled with love that comes from a pure heart, a clear conscience, and genuine faith.

1 TIMOTHY 1:5

Imitate God, therefore, in everything you do, because you are his dear children. Live a life filled with love, following the example of Christ. He loved us and offered himself as a sacrifice for us, a pleasing aroma to God.

EPHESIANS 5:1-2

Let all that you do be done in love.

1 CORINTHIANS 16:14, ESV

Love Is the Answer

In the context of marriage, if we do not feel loved, our differences are magnified. We each come to view the other as a threat to our happiness. We fight for self-worth and significance, and marriage becomes a battlefield rather than a haven.

Love is not the answer to every problem, but it creates a climate of security in which we can seek answers to those issues that bother us. In the security of love, a couple can discuss differences without fear of condemnation. Conflicts can be resolved. Two people who are different can learn to live together in harmony and discover how to bring out the best in each other. Those are the rewards of love.

Love really is the most powerful force in the world. It was love that led Christ to give his life for us. We have eternal life because of his love, and we also have an opportunity to love each other as his representatives. In Ephesians 5, the apostle Paul encourages us to follow Christ's example and live a life of love. Marriages function best when both partners feel genuinely loved. The decision to love your spouse holds tremendous potential, and learning his or her primary love language makes that potential a reality.

Life Promises

Husbands, love your wives and do not be harsh with them.

COLOSSIANS 3:19, NIV

A new commandment I give to you, that you love one another: just as I have loved you, you also are to love one another. By this all people will know that you are my disciples, if you have love for one another.

JOHN 13:34-35, ESV

Husbands ought to love their wives as they love their own bodies. For a man who loves his wife actually shows love for himself.

EPHESIANS 5:28

A Touch of Love

In marriage, the love language of physical touch has many dialects. This does not mean that all touches are created equal. Some will bring more pleasure to your spouse than others. Your best instructor is your spouse. Your wife knows what she perceives as a loving touch; don't insist on touching her in your way and in your time. Respect her wishes. Learn to speak her dialect. Don't make the mistake of believing that the touch that brings pleasure to you will also bring the most pleasure to her.

First Peter 3:7 says that husbands are to dwell with our wives "according to knowledge" (KJV) or "in an understanding way" (ESV). In other words, we need to know our spouse on a deep level. Men, the primary source of knowledge about what makes your wife feel loved is your wife. Some wives enjoy a back rub, others can take it or leave it, and others find it annoying. Women, of course the same goes for husbands.

God made your spouse unique. Physical touch is one of the five love languages, but you must discover what *kind* of touches your spouse enjoys. When you speak the right dialect of physical touch, your loved one will feel loved.

Life Promises

The husband should fulfill his wife's sexual needs, and the wife should fulfill her husband's needs. The wife gives authority over her body to her husband, and the husband gives authority over his body to his wife. Do not deprive each other of sexual relations.

1 CORINTHIANS 7:3-5

Rejoice in the wife of your youth. . . . May you always be captivated by her love.

PROVERBS 5:18-19

We know that for those who love God all things work together for good, for those who are called according to his purpose.

ROMANS 8:28, ESV

Baby Steps

One wife told me, "I want to touch my husband, but when I try, he draws back. He acts like it irritates him, unless of course we are having sex." What is this man telling his wife by his behavior? That physical touch is not his primary love language. He will respond much better to words of affirmation or one of the other love languages. If physical touch is your spouse's primary love language, he or she will welcome tender touches any time you want to give them.

Often, people speak their own love language to others. So if your spouse is always wanting to hug or kiss, it may be because that is what he or she would like from you.

Some people find it difficult to speak the language of physical touch. Perhaps they were not touched as children, and touching is uncomfortable for them. But anyone can learn to speak this language.

Paul makes it clear that we are not to deprive our spouse of sexual intercourse—or any other meaningful touch. When we marry, our bodies are no longer just our own. We can use touch as a gift to each other. Remember, love is about seeking to meet your spouse's need, not your own. You don't touch because it feels comfortable to you but because it communicates love to your beloved.

Life Promises

May the words of my mouth and the meditation of my heart be pleasing to you, O LORD, my rock and my redeemer.

PSALM 19:14

If you need wisdom, ask our generous God, and he will give it to you.

JAMES 1:5

Do not neglect to do good and to share what you have, for such sacrifices are pleasing to God.

HEBREWS 13:16, ESV

That's a Great Question!

Talking is the most fundamental art of marriage—and often the most ignored. How would you respond to this question: "Will you share with me one experience you had today and how it affected you?" How do you think your spouse would respond? Why not ask it and see? Sharing with each other is not that difficult, and it is encouraged by questions.

Questions need to be specific and open ended. "Did you have a good day?" is likely to elicit only a yes or a no. Instead, try, "What were the high and low points in your day and why?" It will take a little reflection, but you and your spouse can answer that question, and your answers may lead to more involved conversations. Questions should not be asked for the purpose of creating an argument, but so that you can understand what is going on in your spouse's life.

Silence leads to isolation and separation. Sharing your thoughts leads to understanding and closeness. Marriage should involve two people having fellowship with each other, not two people living in the same house alone. As we talk, we can pray that our words and conversations would be pleasing to the Lord. Ask a question today, and stimulate meaningful conversation.

Life Promises

The man who finds a wife finds a treasure, and he receives favor from the LORD.

PROVERBS 18:22

Give honor to marriage, and remain faithful to one another in marriage.

HEBREWS 13:4

You husbands must give honor to your wives. Treat your wife with understanding as you live together. She may be weaker than you are, but she is your equal partner in God's gift of new life.

1 PETER 3:7

The Gift of Marriage

The research is in, and marriage is the winner. It's true. Married people are happier, healthier, and more satisfied with life than are singles. It seems that contemporary people are discovering by means of sociological research what the Bible declared to be true thousands of years ago.

It was God who said, "It is not good for the man to be alone" (Genesis 2:18). The first man, Adam, had a vocation. He had a place to live and plenty of animals to pet. He even had a relationship with God. But it was God's analysis that Adam needed a wife. God had created all the animals in pairs—male and female—but had initially created only one human. Eve's creation was not an afterthought. God didn't say, "Oh, I forgot to make a woman. I'd better take care of that." No! It was a matter of timing. God's intention all along was to create people both male and female, but he first wanted to give Adam time to survey the world and discover the need for companionship—a counterpart to himself. Then God created what he termed "a helper who is just right for him."

King Solomon tells us in Proverbs 18 that the man who finds a wife—or, we can extrapolate, the woman who finds a husband—finds a treasure. Marriage is a beautiful gift from the Lord.

Life Promises

[Jesus said,] "I will show you what it's like when someone comes to me, listens to my teaching, and then follows it. It is like a person building a house who digs deep and lays the foundation on solid rock. When the floodwaters rise and break against that house, it stands firm because it is well built."

LUKE 6:47-48

I will make you my wife forever, showing you righteousness and justice, unfailing love and compassion. I will be faithful to you and make you mine, and you will finally know me as the LORD.

HOSEA 2:19-20

Above all, keep loving one another earnestly, since love covers a multitude of sins.

1 PETER 4:8, ESV

Laying a Strong Foundation

A strong foundation is the key to a strong marriage. Jesus told the story of a wise person who built a house on a foundation of solid rock. When storms and floods came, the house was not shaken. Contrast that to the foolish person, who built a house with no foundation. It collapsed at the first storm. The foundation in our relationship with God is faith, trust, and obedience. In our marriage, the foundation is oneness.

In God's plan, marriage involves two people, husband and wife, becoming one unit. They choose to share life more deeply with each other than with anyone else. This intimacy involves all aspects of life. Ideally, before we get married, we should explore the foundation for oneness. Intellectually, are we on the same wavelength? Can we talk and understand each other? Emotionally, are we able to share our feelings without fear of rejection? Socially, do we enjoy similar activities? Spiritually, are we marching to the beat of the same drummer?

After marriage, we build on this foundation. If the foundation is shaky, then it will be more difficult to build intimacy. But build we must, for that is the heart of what marriage is all about. Creating intimacy may be difficult, but we have all of God's help when we commit ourselves to following his plan.

Life Promises

We will speak the truth in love, growing in every way more and more like Christ, who is the head of his body, the church.

EPHESIANS 4:15

Look at those who are honest and good, for a wonderful future awaits those who love peace.

PSALM 37:37

Whatever is true, whatever is honorable, whatever is just, whatever is pure, whatever is lovely, whatever is commendable, if there is any excellence, if there is anything worthy of praise, think about these things.

PHILIPPIANS 4:8, ESV

The Truth about Doves

Marriage experts have discovered some common communication patterns that are detrimental to communication. One such pattern is what is sometimes called the Dove. In this pattern, one partner placates the other in order to avoid his or her wrath. It's the "peace at any price" syndrome. Typical statements from a Dove are, "That's fine with me" or "Whatever makes you happy makes me happy."

Doves are always trying to appease the other person, often apologizing for things that may have upset the partner, no matter how insignificant. They almost never disagree with their spouse openly, no matter how they feel. Often the Dove pattern grows out of low self-esteem. The placater may think, *My ideas are not worth anything, so why express them?* He or she may also fear the spouse's response to disagreement.

It should be obvious that this pattern of communication does not build authentic marriages. Honesty honors God and reflects his image. Psalm 31:5 even refers to the Lord as "the God of truth" (NIV). We must learn to speak the truth, with grace and in love, to be sure, but we must speak the truth.

Life Promises

I have been a constant example of how you can help those in need by working hard. You should remember the words of the Lord Jesus: "It is more blessed to give than to receive."

ACTS 20:35

Give, and it will be given to you. Good measure, pressed down, shaken together, running over, will be put into your lap. For with the measure you use it will be measured back to you.

LUKE 6:38, ESV

Bear one another's burdens, and so fulfill the law of Christ.

GALATIANS 6:2, ESV

The Secret to True Happiness

Happiness is a unique commodity. It is never found by the person shopping for it. Lonely men and women in every age have admitted the futility of their search for happiness, most notably King Solomon in the book of Ecclesiastes. This wealthy, powerful king, with servants to cater to his every whim, found most things in life to be tedious, meaningless, and devoid of joy.

Most of us get married assuming that we are going to be happy. After the wedding, we find that our mate does not always seek to make us happy. Perhaps our spouse even demands more and more of our time, energy, and resources for his or her own happiness. We feel cheated and used, so we fight for our rights. We demand that our spouse do certain things for us, or we give up and seek happiness elsewhere.

Part of the apostle Paul's definition of love in 1 Corinthians 13 is that it is "not self-seeking" (verse 5, NIV). Genuine happiness is the by-product of making someone else happy. I wonder what would have happened if King Solomon had found someone to serve? Don't the Scriptures say, "It is more blessed to give than to receive" (Acts 20:35)?

Do you want to be happy? Discover someone else's needs, and seek to meet them. Why not begin with your spouse? "How may I help you?" is a good question with which to begin.

Life Promises

The Holy Spirit produces this kind of fruit in our lives: love, joy, peace, patience, kindness, goodness, faithfulness, gentleness, and self-control. There is no law against these things!

GALATIANS 5:22-23

I say, love your enemies! Pray for those who persecute you! In that way, you will be acting as true children of your Father in heaven. For he gives his sunlight to both the evil and the good, and he sends rain on the just and the unjust alike. If you love only those who love you, what reward is there for that? Even corrupt tax collectors do that much. If you are kind only to your friends, how are you different from anyone else? Even pagans do that. But you are to be perfect, even as your Father in heaven is perfect.

MATTHEW 5:44-48

Since God chose you to be the holy people he loves, you must clothe yourselves with tenderhearted mercy, kindness, humility, gentleness, and patience. Make allowance for each other's faults, and forgive anyone who offends you. Remember, the Lord forgave you, so you must forgive others.

COLOSSIANS 3:12-13

The Transforming Power of Love

The story is told of a woman who went to a marriage counselor for advice. "I want to divorce my husband," she said, "and I want to hurt him as much as I can."

"In that case," the counselor advised, "start showering him with compliments. When you have become indispensable to him—when he thinks you love him devotedly—then start the divorce action. That's the way to hurt him most."

Some months later, the wife returned to report that she had followed the counselor's advice.

"Good," said the counselor. "Now's the time to file for divorce."

"Divorce?" said the woman. "Never! I've fallen in love with the guy."

Loving words and actions change not only the spouse; they change the one speaking and acting lovingly. Didn't Jesus say, "Love your enemies" (Matthew 5:44)? Perhaps your spouse qualifies, at least at certain moments! It may seem impossible, but Galatians 5 reassures us that it's not all up to us. The Holy Spirit, who dwells within believers, produces godly attributes in us: love, joy, peace, patience, kindness, goodness, faithfulness, gentleness, and self-control. All we need to do is allow him to work within us.

Loving your spouse in the power of the Holy Spirit will never make things worse. Who knows? Things may get better. Go against your emotions, and give love a chance.

Life Promises

Love is not jealous or boastful or proud or rude. It does not demand its own way. It is not irritable, and it keeps no record of being wronged.

1 CORINTHIANS 13:4-5

Get rid of all bitterness, rage, anger, harsh words, and slander, as well as all types of evil behavior. Instead, be kind to each other, tenderhearted, forgiving one another, just as God through Christ has forgiven you.

EPHESIANS 4:31-32

The LORD is compassionate and merciful, slow to get angry and filled with unfailing love.

PSALM 103:8

Can't We All Just Get Along?

Why do people argue? In one word, rigidity. When we argue, in essence we are saying, "My way is the right way. If you don't do it my way, I'll make your life miserable." The arguer insists on getting his or her own way.

Conflict resolvers have a different attitude. They say, "I'm sure we can work this out in a way that will be positive for both of us. Let's think about it together." They look for a win-win resolution. They begin by respecting each other's ideas and looking for a solution instead of trying to win an argument.

The Scriptures say that love "does not demand its own way." Love is not proud, either, so it doesn't consider its way best. Actually, love means looking out for the other person's interests. Philippians 2:4 says, "Don't look out only for your own interests, but take an interest in others, too." What would be best for you? is the question of love.

Life Promises

Let the Spirit renew your thoughts and attitudes. Put on your new nature, created to be like God—truly righteous and holy.

EPHESIANS 4:23-24

Great is his faithfulness; his mercies begin afresh each morning.

LAMENTATIONS 3:23

Anyone who belongs to Christ has become a new person. The old life is gone; a new life has begun!

2 CORINTHIANS 5:17

It's Not You, It's Me

Is your personality an asset or a liability to your marriage? Most personality traits are expressed by contrasting words. We speak of an individual being optimistic or pessimistic, critical or complimentary, extroverted or introverted, patient or impatient. While our personalities are developed in childhood, they are not set in concrete. We can change.

If I realize that my tendency to withdraw and remain silent is detrimental to my marriage, I can learn to share my feelings and thoughts. If I realize that my critical attitude is killing my mate's spirit, I can break the pattern and learn to give compliments.

The message of the Bible is that God loves us as we are, but he loves us too much to leave us as we are. We all need to grow, and growth requires change. We are influenced by our personalities, but we need not be controlled by them. Instead, we are to be controlled by the Holy Spirit. In Ephesians 4, Paul tells us to "let the Spirit renew [our] thoughts and attitudes." He will work in our lives, but we need to allow him to do it. When we yield to him, we will see significant changes in our approaches to life and marriage.

Life Promises

Be an example to all believers in what you say, in the way you live, in your love, your faith, and your purity.

1 TIMOTHY 4:12

Christ will make his home in your hearts as you trust in him. Your roots will grow down into God's love and keep you strong. And may you have the power to understand, as all God's people should, how wide, how long, how high, and how deep his love is. May you experience the love of Christ, though it is too great to understand fully. Then you will be made complete with all the fullness of life and power that comes from God.

EPHESIANS 3:17-19

Surely your goodness and unfailing love will pursue me all the days of my life.

PSALM 23:6

A Legacy of Love

What kind of legacy will you leave your children? When you die, you will leave some material legacy: money, clothes, furniture, cars, and so forth. But the most powerful legacy you will leave your children is the legacy of your marriage.

John buried his seventy-eight-year-old father a year after his mother passed away. His father had lived in a nursing home for several years, and his money had run out. He had no financial legacy to leave. "Before he died," John recalled, "he told me he wanted me to have his wedding band. After his death, when I went to the nursing home, they gave me a bag with Dad's clothes. At the bottom was a small plastic bag containing his wedding band. Now that ring is on my dresser. I look at it every day and remind myself of Dad's faithful marriage to Mom for over fifty years. I think about all he did for me when I was young, and I pray that I will be the kind of husband and father he was."

John's words speak of a legacy far more valuable than material property. The apostle Paul wrote to Timothy, encouraging him to be an example in the way he lived, believed, and loved. That's a challenge to us as well. What will your children think someday when they look at your wedding ring?

Scripture Index

About the Author

Dr. Gary Chapman is the author of the perennial bestseller *The Five Love Languages* (more than 4 million copies sold) and numerous other marriage and family books. He also coauthored a fiction series based on *The Four Seasons of Marriage* with bestselling author Catherine Palmer. Dr. Chapman is the director of Marriage and Family Life Consultants, Inc.; an internationally known speaker; and the host of *A Love Language Minute*, a syndicated radio program heard on more than two hundred stations across North America. He and his wife, Karolyn, live in North Carolina.

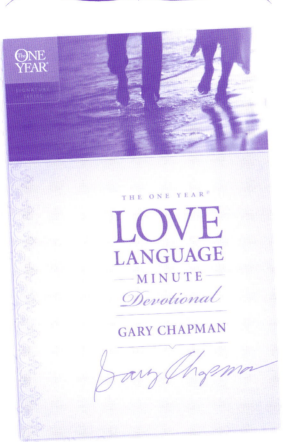